D1548102

LOVING JUSTICE, LIVING SHAKESPEARE

To Brittany
with all
Good Wishes
for your own work!
Regan Schalk
'18

LOVING JUSTICE,
Living Shakespeare

REGINA MARA
SCHWARTZ

OXFORD
UNIVERSITY PRESS

OXFORD
UNIVERSITY PRESS

Great Clarendon Street, Oxford, OX2 6DP,
United Kingdom

Oxford University Press is a department of the University of Oxford.
It furthers the University's objective of excellence in research, scholarship,
and education by publishing worldwide. Oxford is a registered trade mark of
Oxford University Press in the UK and in certain other countries

© Regina Mara Schwartz 2016

The moral rights of the author have been asserted

First Edition published in 2016

Impression: 1

All rights reserved. No part of this publication may be reproduced, stored in
a retrieval system, or transmitted, in any form or by any means, without the
prior permission in writing of Oxford University Press, or as expressly permitted
by law, by licence or under terms agreed with the appropriate reprographics
rights organization. Enquiries concerning reproduction outside the scope of the
above should be sent to the Rights Department, Oxford University Press, at the
address above

You must not circulate this work in any other form
and you must impose this same condition on any acquirer

Published in the United States of America by Oxford University Press
198 Madison Avenue, New York, NY 10016, United States of America

British Library Cataloguing in Publication Data
Data available

Library of Congress Control Number: 2016952145

ISBN 978–0–19–879521–6

Printed in Great Britain by
Clays Ltd, St Ives plc

To Sandro
with infinite love,

"the more I give to thee, the more I have"
—Romeo and Juliet 2. 2.134

Foreword by Rowan Williams

What might it be to see the world 'justly'? Our usual language about justice doesn't seem to help at all in answering, or even understanding, such a question. We have become used to thinking about justice as a matter of discharging clearly defined 'debts'—just as we have increasingly come to see rights as a matter of satisfying clearly defined claims. Justice is sometimes opposed to 'charity' in our political and social discourse: it is supposed to provide hard rather than soft imperatives, to deliver us from sentimentality and condescension. Relieving poverty or suffering ceases to be a gratuitous and generous action that brings honour to the agent, and is reconfigured in the prosaic but honest terms of simply rectifying a balance or compensating for an injury.

There are important insights here, of course. We don't want to perpetuate an attitude which privileges the status of the generous giver in a way that takes our eyes off the question of how and why we got into a situation where such action needed to be taken. We don't want to settle with a picture of charity as the ultimate emotional tool of power. We are rightly eager to emphasize the fact that what is given to the needy is what is *due*, not a kindly bonus. Yet this language alone leaves us feeling that we have missed some crucial point. Regina Schwartz, in this moving, subtle, and impassioned book, helps us see that talking about justice without talking about the quality of human relating is not just vacuous but profoundly dangerous, making us crassly insensitive to how we manage our encounters with actual human need, pain, and crisis. And to connect this sense of unease with the need for us to learn how to see truthfully and lovingly is one of the tasks this book addresses.

This is where Shakespeare's dramas come in. Shakespeare shows us repeatedly what it is to *fail* in justice: which is not to fail to do what we ought, in the narrow sense of leaving debts unpaid, but a failure to see and to communicate—and to let oneself *be* seen and communicated with. This is what love has to do with justice, because this seeing and communicating requires an embeddedness within trust and patience which can manage the profound risk of exposure to one another. We can see justly and do justice—in the rich and complex biblical sense of this phrase—when we grasp that truth will not kill us; or if it does, it kills the evasive, rivalrous, myth-making self that imprisons us in inequity and violence. Shakespeare neither reduces love to positive emotion nor renders justice as the exact payment of debt. He makes both ideas denser and more unfamiliar by weaving them brilliantly together, and so sketching a picture of what is fundamentally *human* in both. Love is intensely demanding in precise particulars; justice is about debts that can never be paid. And in so doing, he helps us formulate a set of necessary challenges to our current fictions about medical care, about economic life, about penal policies and their goals, and about entire political systems. Regina Schwartz's close readings especially of *The Merchant of Venice* and *Romeo and Juliet* draw out in detail how reflection on love can prompt the most far-reaching political and economic questions, laying bare the starkness of all alternatives to just love and loving justice.

This is a study of unusual breadth and freshness, in which insights from literature, psychology, philosophy, and personal experience are woven tightly together. At a time when we are assailed by a variety of temptations to moral short cuts, to impatience with the full depth of what is to be 'seen' in human beings, it is timely, humane and radical.

—R.W., Master of Magdalene College at the University of Cambridge, 104th Archbishop of Canterbury, and author of *The Tragic Imagination*.

Acknowledgements

A project that takes ten years incurs much gratitude. My chief intellectual debts are to Nicholas Wolterstorff and Charles Taylor whose important works on justice are marked not only by great rigor but by values I consider essential to thinking through justice. Both their work and frequent substantive conversations with them provided me with a vital sense of community as I wrote this.

My special thanks to the Institute for Advanced Study of Culture in Charlottesville, Virginia, where I was privileged to be a Fellow and participate in a reading group on Justice. My thanks to the Law students at Northwestern University Law School who filled my course on "Ideas of Justice" for six years and asked penetrating questions, and to the remarkable graduate students in the Academy for Advanced Study of the Renaissance for thoughtful conversations about Shakespeare. Special thanks to Andrew Keener and Patrick McGrath for their generous help.

I want to thank the University of Pisa Department of Philosophy for the opportunity to lecture to their graduate students on justice in Aristotle and Shakespeare, the Humanities Institute at Johns Hopkins University for the opportunity to offer two chapters in progress, the Fetzer Institute for the chance to contribute to their symposium on punishment and forgiveness, the Castelli Philosophy Colloquium in Rome for the opportunity to present my thoughts on scarcity, the Kingston Shakespeare Series in London, and the Shakespeare Institute in Stratford-upon-Avon for helping with my thoughts on *The Merchant of Venice*, Harvard University Divinity School for the invitation to respond to Rowan Williams with my work on Lear and Love, UCLA's Shakespeare Conference for the chance to share thoughts on *Hamlet*, and the University of California Santa Barbara's Department of Religious Studies for inviting me to give their annual Tipton Chair address on forgiveness. My debt to Michael Crawford is of another kind: his work became my prose model as I boldly inserted myself into this story of justice and love. Thanks to Ken Seeskin for arguing with me about Kant for many happy hours. My gratitude to Bill Davis and Ed Muir is beyond words.

Earlier segments or versions of a few of the chapters have been published in several journals and books:

"On Religion and Literature: Truth, Beauty and the Good," co-authored with Vittorio Montemaggi, *Journal of Religion and Literature*, 2015; "Monotheism and Scarcity," in *Archivio di filosofia: consacré à la question du 'monothéisme,'* 2014; "Revenge, Forgiveness, and Love," in *Love and Forgiveness for a More Just World*, ed. Hent de Vries and Nils F. Schott, Columbia University Press, 2014; "Loving Justice," *English Language Notes*, Special Issue on Scriptural Margins, 50/2 (2012), 23–40; "Law and the Gift of Justice," in *Crediting God: Sovereignty and Religion in the Age of Global Capitalism*, ed. Miguel Vatter, Fordham University Press, 2011; "Grave Images: Terror and Justice," in *Theology and the Soul of the Liberal State*, ed. Leonard V. Kaplan and Charles L. Cohen, Rowman and Littlefield Publishers, 2010; "The Price of Justice and Love in *The Merchant of Venice*," *Triquarterly*, Spring 2006, rpt. in *Shakespeare Criticism*, Thomson, 2007; "Law and Love in *The Merchant of Venice*," in *Practising Equity, Addressing Law: Equity in Law and Literature*, ed. Daniela Carpi, Anglistische Forschungen, 2008; "The Violence of Idolatry," *The Bible and Critical Theory*, 4/1 (2008), 2.1–2.7; "Revelation and Idolatry: Holy Law and Holy Terror," *Genre*, 40, 3–4 (2007), 1–16; "Revelation and Revolution," in *Theology and the Political*, ed. Creston Davis, Duke University Press, 2005; "The Revelation of Justice," in *Derrida and Religion: Other Testaments*, ed. Yvonne Sherwood and Kevin Hart, Routledge, 2004.

Contents

Contents

I

The Experience of Love

Love talks with better knowledge, and knowledge with dearer love.
SHAKESPEARE, *Measure for Measure*

Lessons of Mother Love

I was holding her hand and singing softly to her when the man in the white coat came in. I guessed from his coldness that he was not bearing good news. Sometimes, when I was surrounded by doctors who had given up on Mama's life, I felt besieged by a death squad. When she was alert, her warm brown reassuring eyes could make me move mountains, certainly strengthen me to ward off their negativity. But when she was in a medicated sleep, I was on my own and more vulnerable. Now here was the ominous pulmonologist. He beckoned me to the window, held up both sets of X-rays, and showed that the dark area was bigger on today's films than yesterday's: her lungs were filling up with fluid. I suspected this was a side-effect from one of the drugs this hospital had introduced for her infection. So, looking at those dark shadows in the X-rays at the window, I went on "side-effect alert." This meant that immediately I would need to search reliable computer sites like the Mayo Clinic or Harvard Med about drug reactions, consult with specialists, and stop whatever was encroaching in my mother's lungs immediately. However, this doctor seemed to have another plan.

I discovered what that was two hours later, when another man appeared in her room, this one clad in a dark suit instead of a white jacket. Dark-suit had been sent by White-jacket to speak to me about "the question of life." I asked what his specialty was, doubting that he was a philosopher. "Ethics" he said, and then, to my horror, he began telling me—in front of my mother—that there were questions about the quality of her life. Some ethicist. I put my finger over my lips to implore his silence, and whispered that any such conversation surely needed to take place elsewhere. In the hall, I explained that I too am very interested in ethics and that I'd been teaching courses in Justice and Ethics at the Northwestern Law School. He replied me that he was an expert in *medical* Ethics. So now, it seemed, I needed to turn from side-effects to ethics alert.

In the end, our conversation was surprisingly short, and not nearly as philosophical as I anticipated. He gave me a list of my mother's disabilities—as if I didn't know—and then concluded that they added up to the end of her life. Some kind of ethics. I didn't need to save my mother in a protracted philosophical battle on ethics, only to punch him out. You see, I had heard the phrase "we can make her comfortable" intoned with gravitas one too many times. Now I was more disappointed than devastated when doctors wanted to kill my mother. She had recovered from her first stroke, compensating for the losses on one side of her brain with the other side. Through the tireless work of specialists at the Chicago Rehabilitation Institute and her own determination, she had regained virtually all of her capacities. Then, a year later, the second stroke cruelly hit the functioning side of her brain. The damage was motor: she couldn't walk, talk, or swallow any more. But she could still paint and she was an artist: her right arm was spared, still mobile and very strong. She could reason clearly and had a rich emotional life. She could communicate effectively, writing when she needed, but what she mainly communicated, through her eyes, was love.

I periodically asked her if her immobility was too hard on her, and did she understand the question. No, she shook her head, it was not too hard on her and yes, she nodded, she understood. I confess I was surprised by her determination, her fortitude, her courage. I sang love songs to her, thankfully, with the help of Plácido Domingo's record-ings. She used her good arm, first to hug me whenever I entered her room, and then to conduct while Plácido and I sang our hearts out.

At the high C's, she would lift her arm to the ceiling, as would I, and our hands would lock there: "esperaaaanza!" When I wasn't singing along with the Maestro, I read to her, assisted her painting, shared magazine ads with her (we had been critiquing advertising layouts since I was a child), and told her silly stories and laughed with her. We did not worry about the news, or errands, or who we liked and didn't or why. We just loved. Days flew by.

When she sickened, we went together in the ambulance to whatever doctors or hospitals she needed. Nursing her was not draining because she was always giving so much. What she gave was what she always gave, a level of understanding that is beyond words. And not just to me. After her first stroke, in rehab class, Nurse Mary had arranged the wheelchairs of the patients in a circle and was batting a balloon to each in order. When the balloon fell to just the right level for that patient's capacities, she would call out "now" and the patient's motionless arm would reach and try to hit it. Watching her level of acute observation, I felt like I was finally learning how to teach. Only one patient, a paraplegic teenager who had been shot in gang warfare, didn't try. My mother could talk then, and she rolled her chair up to him and quietly said, "If I am trying to do this, and I am in my late eighties, then you really ought to give it your best." He did after that.

Now, a young nurse stopped me in the hospital just before Darksuit appeared: "Aren't you Regina? How is your mother? You know, I owe my new job to her: she encouraged me to learn to drive, so I would be not at the mercy of agencies with vans and I could get to the hospital to work. I love working here." My mother had sprinkled her fairy dust on this woman, as on everyone else she knew.

So, I told Mr Ethics: "Quality of life? My mother cannot run a mile or eat a meal at a table, but she is giving and receiving more love than anyone in this place who can. I'm not sure how you measure quality of life, but that is how we do." His eyes instantly welled up with tears and he walked away, apparently unable to speak.

Indeed, one of the side-effects of her new drug was fluid in the lungs, and once we stopped that medication, Mama's lungs began to clear. But first, I had to ask for a new pulmonologist who had a richer sense of life's quality. And that meant we had to move hospitals. We did, and we lived and loved for three more years together.

It is a curious fact that while whole sectors of our culture are preoccupied with love—novels, film, painting, music, poetry, religion—it has been marginalized or even exiled from other spheres—from political, economic, legal thought, and largely, even from philosophy. Somehow love is regarded as a "soft" subject, fit for the arts and fine for private life, but not for the tough business of the public sphere, of making hard choices, negotiating power, and forging contracts. So, the hospital's expert on ethics was making calculations, mostly economic ones (the cost to the hospital of keeping this patient alive), utilitarian ones (the greatest good for the greatest number, not for those who are outside the majority), and to be fair to him, calculations about her functionality— could she achieve her goals and pursue the excellence of "living well" that society has defined for the elderly (from playing golf to travelling). With all of this preoccupation with utility, it is no wonder that love was not even on his radar screen.

Why is love regarded as the highest human value in some cultural sectors and not even on the map in others? Make no mistake, for many thinkers in many times, love is the very purpose of life. Leviticus in the Hebrew Bible, Jesus in the New Testament, Socrates in the *Symposium*, Aquinas in the *Summa Theologica*, Shakespeare in *King Lear*: for each of them, love defines us as human. Loving is not only our deepest nature, it is also the goal of all of life's experiences. From *La Bohème* to the Beatles, from *Sabrina* to *Star Wars*, from *Antigone* to *Anna Karenina*, both high and pop culture underscore the priority of love. And yet, in my office where several bookshelves are devoted to books on political theories of justice, not even one has a chapter on love.[1] Justice is deemed a political, public concern, while love is personal and private.

Conversely, the books on religion are full of it. In those, love comes in different names depending on who is loving, who is loved, and how they are loved: caritas, agape, eros, altruism, divine love, neighbor love. In these books, love is not just a private emotion, but preeminently public—it is social glue, and more, it is virtually tantamount to justice.

I was already knee deep wading through theories of justice for my course when my mother had her first stroke. I had already begun to suspect that the really helpful theories of justice had been articulated in religious discourse, that nothing higher had been thought than that justice *was* love, as when the Hebrew Bible said love your neighbor (Lev. 19:18) and love the stranger (Deut. 10:19, Lev. 19:33–5); when the New Testament added love your enemy, and when Jesus confirmed that all the law was summed up in the command to love, and the rabbis agreed that he had gotten that right (Matt. 22:37–40, Mark 12:28–31, Luke 10:25–8). And I worried that philosophy and political thought, with their preoccupations with distribution, duty, and rights, had not fully wrestled with this rich love tradition. It seemed that this tradition, of love as justice, was lost.

But it was when Dark-suit, the ethics expert, had not even considered love as what is worth living for, that I began to consider how mistaken political, economic, and philosophical thought were for shifting the focus away from love. If my mother's life, chock full of love, did not already have apparent value to an ethicist, and conversely, if the lives of accomplished able-bodied medical professionals could so quickly be exposed as impoverished when loveless, then clearly, love needed to be reconsidered.

Justice: What's Love Got to Do With It?

To judge by most ethical and political thought, nothing. Most often, we speak of Justice as if it were tangibly real, even as if Justice were always somehow with us—ever-watchful. Our conscience is alert to her, knowing that justice demands consideration at all times and in all contexts, from the smallest transaction in personal relationships to the governance of states and global institutions. Even the cosmos is supposed to answer to her. But what is this imaginary that haunts us called Justice? What do the experts say? Any broad sweep of philosophy for answers will necessarily simplify complex thinkers, but the subject of justice compels us to try to draw the bigger picture.

Some define justice as the rather chilly demand for equal distribution. Others describe justice as fair distribution of either goods or opportunities—and equality and fairness are not the same. Equal means that justice isn't satisfied until everybody gets the same. But hardly anybody believes that, so there are other systems of distribution, according to merit and according to need—and those two are not the same. Scholarships are given to the best students at some places, to the neediest at others; hardly any place gives out equal financial packages and hardly any workplace pays all of its employees the same wage. Instead, there are complicated computations made about what is fair— such as equal pay for equal work, greater pay for more work or greater pay for more expertise or greater pay for work that is in more demand. In this way, inequities come to be regarded as not equal, but "equit*able*," and hence as satisfying the demands of justice.

Some regard fairness as equality of opportunities for all: John Rawls, the influential theorist of justice, asks that we completely bracket our social position, our wants and needs, when we craft our idea of fairness. While this sounds intuitively right, it has been roundly critiqued: first, how is it possible to retain one's subjectivity with no embedded social context—family ties, work obligations, personal history? To don the Rawlsian "veil of ignorance" would be to suspend these ties, to do without a substantial identity when making ethical choices. But can we bracket out what is fair from the lives we lead? Secondly, his theory of justice is focused on the individual. But the pursuit of justice needs to include the pursuit of social good, which includes people having different roles in society, and contributing in different ways. Literal equality turns out not to be egalitarian at all if people have different abilities and interests. A pedestrian example: if all children are given the same curriculum out of fairness but some are quite artistic and others more verbal, it may not be fair to induce equal development of both; instead, a curriculum emphasizing arts will be more propitious for one, letters for another. Social justice may require diversity, not sameness. It turns out that political and philosophical thought on the subject is not as helpful as we might anticipate. There are wonderful ideas, many persuasive, and most are worked out quite systematically, but the difficulty is that they conflict with each other, so that no single clear definition of justice has emerged.

There are other factors that govern the justice imaginary, and they are also contested. Some thinkers focus less on equity than on desert, and they interpret the maxim on justice from classical law courts—"to render to each person what is due" to mean to give to each person what he deserves. This kind of thinking conflicts with those who insist on equality or even equitability, as well as those who insist that all have equal dignity and all are equally deserving. These are questions about the person who is the subject of justice and about how to evaluate their personhood fairly in order to know how to treat him justly. But there is also the problem of what it is that should be fairly distributed. What is the good that humans strive to attain? Material reward, excellence at some skill, recognition, power, influence, honor? What do we owe one another?[2] Guarantees against harm of our person and our property? The right to life? There are those who say we owe each other those rights and far more; they find rights theories alone too minimal. Only a few radical thinkers have said that love is the supreme good, that we even owe each other love, or that there can be no justice without love.

Religious understandings of justice differ markedly from political and philosophical thought on distribution. Broadly speaking, the biblical traditions suggest that what we most value is a free gift given from an infinite supply. The primary good sought is love, and the more of it you give, the more it is replenished. It is not in scarce supply, but limitless. This usually does not presuppose exchange; rather, love is a gift given without any expectation of return, freely given. Clearly, when love is added to the mix of thought on distribution, something very jarring occurs. The entire bedrock of distribution, as based upon a limited supply, is cracked open. From the perspective of love, nature is self-renewing, the energy of life is unlimited, even if individuals themselves die, and even if you cannot get everything all at once, our world is abundant. If distributive justice is governed by scarcity thinking—we must figure out how to share the limited supply we have—the biblical picture of justice is far different: we can hope for more and give more of what we most need—love.

"Love the stranger," as it says in Deuteronomy 10:19, may be one of the most challenging ideas in the history of western ethical thought. Some (including Freud) thought it was incoherent. Love the stranger may as well signify love someone from Mars. How can I love such a person? But the deep wisdom of that injunction is precisely to value someone with whom we have no ties, no relations, no basis of trust, no preconceptions of a shared worldview, no prior communication, and hence, absolutely no way of assessing, let alone appreciating him. *This* is the person we must value, we must love, simply because he is a person. That is enough. As a person, he richly deserves to be appreciated. This is not the value of achievement, but the intrinsic value that a human person has that is far deeper than the superficial value of performance. All people have this fundamental value and in this sense all are lovable.

One difficulty with the command to love the stranger for some (including Kant), is the assumption that love cannot be commanded, but as the philosopher Raimond Gaita has pointed out, we *can* be required to love better: "Love has its standards and lovers must try to rise to them."[3] He continues,

The standards intrinsic to love in all its forms are partly an expression of respect for the independent reality of the beloved. To the eye of a moralist, that can look like a straightforwardly moral requirement, independent of love as a passion. It is half true. We would not have a sense of the independent reality of the beloved if we did not think of her as someone who could be wronged. But we would not have the sense of her as someone who could be wronged, if we did not have a sense of her as precious in a way that has largely been conditioned by the language of love. The requirements of love and those of morality are, I believe, interdependent...[4]

For him, we cannot speak of obligations to a person without the assumption that they are precious, lovable. Throughout Gaita's work, the insight surfaces that love reveals the value of a person—in the sense of uncovers, makes apparent, as in a revelation. He asserts, "Our talk of rights is dependent on the works of love."[5] And so, I would add, is our talk of duty and fairness. Gaita's profound insights into the interdependence of love and morality are rare today.[6] But here I want to revive that ancient religious understanding of justice, one encoded in the simple commands to love the neighbor and to love the stranger. As I will show, that understanding has been kept alive, if not in political thought, in the world of a much-beloved playwright.

How did that medical ethicist arrive at the calculus that my mother should die? Did he really think that a feeling thinking being was disposable because she was unable to walk? Or was he making an economic calculus, that to treat her lungs to make her well, to keep a bedridden person alive, was costly, and perhaps he was even more utilitarian than that, and calculated that my mother could not give society what a working person could (should we kill all the retirees?) and that because she was elderly, she should not take up a place in the sun any more. He certainly did not "calculate" her infinite love, the way it transformed everyone who came in contact with her: not only her family and friends but also each nurse, each fellow rehab patient, and even the ambulance drivers. And he didn't calculate what effects their being loved in turn wrought on others. In this light, the perils of separating justice from love come into full view. The dangers of this separation are serious indeed. Human life is reduced to cost–benefit analyses, to mutual benefit at best, and to individual benefit more frequently. Down the slippery slope of protecting self-interest, all forms of caring for any reason other than self-enhancement are effectively expunged from the map. Can we do better?

Justice: What's Reason Got to Do With It?

Most concepts of justice celebrate reason. Ever since Plato, the idea that reason must govern the unruly passions has taken hold. The rule of reason is encoded in that vivid image in *The Phaedrus* of the charioteer who must curb his wild steeds of passion and the will in order to set his rational course. Ever since, the priority of reason story says that when humans succumb to passions, they are anything but just. Their lives are "brutish, nasty"—Hobbes's language—for they are selfish, competitive, and prone to violence. Thucydides said this forcefully when he was describing the horrors of the Peloponnesian war: "The cause of all these evils," he said, "was the lust for power arising from greed and ambition, and from these passions proceeded the violence of the parties." Hobbes translated him, endorsing his view of human nature even as he recommended a different solution for its faults: "the dispositions of men are naturally such, that except they be restrained through fear of some coercive power, every man will distrust and dread every other and as by natural right he may, so by necessity he will be forced to make use of the strength he has, towards the preservation of himself."[7]

This dark anthropology is ancient: even four centuries before Thucydides, Hesiod spoke in his *Works and Days* of the human lust for power:

> Father will have no common bond with son,
> Neither will guest with host, nor friend with friend;
> The brother-love of past days will be gone.
>
> .   .   .   .
>
> Might will be right, and shame
> Will cease to be. . . .
>   And everywhere
> Harsh-voiced and sullen-faced and loving harm,
> Envy will walk along with wretched men.

And it is remarkably tenacious: in eighteenth-century America, John Adams read both Thucydides and Hobbes and while he replaced the Hobbesian political solution of monarchy with republicanism, he also understood human nature as aggressively self-interested. Again, the human passions continued to fare poorly under the scrutiny of Kant, who defines the moral act as one governed by reason and not inclination, and whose influence on contemporary critical thinkers is difficult to overstate. The standard story tells us that at its best, reason allows us to formulate ideas about justice, to cultivate a sphere of law to enforce justice, and to design communities founded on principles of justice. Reason dictates that such justice will be founded on concepts of fairness, impartiality, and just measure, concepts that can be universalized.

Measurement will not only govern the way we distribute goods, services, and opportunities, but also the way we mete out punishment. That way, retribution is neither too great nor too little with regard to the crime, but "just right"—like Goldilocks and the Three Bears. Not Goldilocks, in fact, but Aristotle is responsible for this widespread understanding of justice as just measurement. Like Plato, Aristotle has respect for love—it emerges in his discussion of the importance of friendship—but when he writes explicitly about justice, he turns to the language of measure, making distribution vital to our thinking about justice.

In his *Nicomachean Ethics*, Aristotle associates justice with just proportion, measurement, and, for disparate goods, commensurability, and he defines the judge as the one who divides equally.

"Now the judge restores equality; it is as though there were a line divided into unequal parts, and he took away that by which the greater segment exceeds the half, and added it to the smaller segment. And when the whole has been equally divided, then they say they have 'their own'—i.e. when they have got what is equal."

Indeed, the etymology of the judge is the bisector: "It is for this reason also that it is called just (*dikaion*), because it is a division into two equal parts (*dicha*), just as if one were to call it *dichaion*; and the judge (*dikastes*) is one who bisects (*dichastes*)." If this sounds like a cold definition of a judge, it is. The preoccupation with just measure has also endured: in the iconography, justice is holding scales.[8]

This understanding of justice presupposes that goods can be measured, exchanged in proportion, and that such exchange is the basis of social intercourse; moreover, these goods are finite. Indeed, the most sought commodities, like honor or wealth, are in scarce supply. Not only are goods measurable, so are acts, so that it is possible to create a price for injury and require compensation for it. A deep debt to this understanding of justice, stressing measurement and proportionality, is evident throughout legal systems with economic models of justice. Furthermore, most ideas of fairness in political and ethical thought rely on an understanding of some proportional distribution.[9] A long illustrious line of distribution thinkers, including not only Aristotle, but also Kant and more recently Rawls, have shown us the way to fair distribution. Why do they not fill the heart with the sense that the world will be right—that all injustice will just wither away—if only everyone obeys their deeply thought and well-respected principles? What is missing with these dominant preoccupations with measure? Why do they seem so cold, so minimal—not wrong, but insufficient?

That may be because, first of all, they are light years from the logic of love. Again, with love, the good sought is not in scarce supply, indeed, it is not finite. Its distribution is not a problem because the more of it you give, the more you have to give. Love does not presuppose a cost; rather, it is given freely. Love does not depend on a contract; indeed, contracts are only necessary where love fails. Calvin echoes an entire biblical tradition when he writes that the proof that we serve God is that we serve our neighbors without regard to our cost and labor. He scorns "hirelings" who only help for profit.

God (to try the love which we bear him) offers us such persons as have no means to recompense us. For behold the true proof that we serve God, is that we serve our neighbors when they have neither pleasured nor helped us afore, or when it shall seem that we have lost both our labor and our cost, & yet notwithstanding cease not to employ our selves still.... whensoever we see any poor men in adversity or mistreated, (as when some are in necessity for want of worldly goods, some are wrested and wronged by other men, some stand in need of counsel, and others lack help:) then doth God mean to try our charity, then putteth he us to the touchstone: and if we shrink aside when the poor cryeth, and give no ear to him: thereby we show that we are neither zealous nor willing to serve God.

Despite the centrality of such values to western religious thought, governments, economies, and legal systems have only carved out a very little place for love, decidedly at the margins, and called it charity.[10] As Timothy Jackson puts it, charity, love, agape, concern for the well-being of the other—these are considered supererogatory in the tradition of political thought, over and above the call of duty. And justice is, as Kant intoned, about duty.

Although the "sentiments," as emotions were called, assumed center-stage in the thought of the Scottish Enlightenment philosophers—Hutcheson, Hume, Smith, and Ferguson—Kant definitively separated emotion from reason, taking what had been, at best, the marginal position of love in theories of justice and denied even that, exiling emotion from the moral law altogether. Kant turned his back largely on human experience and emotion to embrace an abstract law founded on "pure reason." He writes in his *Groundwork for the Metaphysics of Morals*:

Is it not a matter of utmost importance to forge for once a pure moral philosophy, completely cleansed of everything that may be only empirical and that really belongs to anthropology?...Consequently, the ground of obligation must here be sought, not in the nature of human beings or in facts about the way the world is, but solely a priori and [by] concepts of pure reason...the metaphysics of morals has to examine the idea and the principles of a possible pure will, and not the acts and conditions of human volition generally, which are drawn largely from psychology.

Our affections, emotions, and inclinations (the stuff of psychology) have at best a subordinate role to the pure principles which should guide us. Kant is careful to distinguish obedience to the law out of respect for the law from inclination: "now if an action done out of duty is supposed to exclude totally the influence of inclination, and, along with inclination, every object of volition, then nothing remains that could determine the will except objectively *the law* and subjectively *pure respect* for this practical law." For him, the moral law must be universal, impartial, and to achieve that, it must leave behind all inclination. We obey the moral law out of duty, not because we are so-inclined. "Duty! What origin is there worthy of thee, and where is to be found the root of thy noble descent which proudly rejects all kinship with the inclinations?" (1788: 89). His ethics are "either uncontaminanted by sensible desires or bereft of feeling, depending upon the perspective."[11]

Kant draws a firm line between love and beneficence: the first is a mere feeling and the second a duty. For him, we are not beneficent toward the neighbor because we love him. We are good to him out of duty.

> Unselfish benevolence towards human beings is often (though very inappro-priately) also called love; people even speak of love which is also a duty for us when it is not a question of another's happiness but of the complete and free surrender of all one's ends to the ends of another (even a supernatural) being. But every duty is a necessitation, a constraint... What is done from constraint, however, is not done from love.[12]

Since Kant, many have written persuasively about the importance of a universal understanding of justice. Without it, how could we correct abuses of human rights? If our understanding of justice is only commu-nal, on what basis can we claim that a given community's endorsement of slavery, or abuse of women, or child-labor is wrong? Because we understand justice to be a universal value of impartiality, all persons, whatever differences of race, gender, religion, or abilities, deserve to be treated with impartiality. The Kantian ideals of universality and impar-tiality have informed theories of justice as fairness, and this includes, more robustly, distribution not only of goods but of opportunities.[13] There are other candidates for a universal ethical theory: not only distri-bution, impartiality, but also a commitment to mutually agreed upon contracts or the attractions of universal human rights.

To be sure, all of these—impartiality, rights, and duties—are enor-mous advances over theories of mutual advantage, homo economicus, or utilitarianism, for in these later economic theories that privilege the greatest number, the marginal invariably suffer. But strangely, even these more advanced versions of justice are built upon the same nega-tive assumption: that humans are self-serving, competitive, and brutal by nature and so their inclinations for self-advancement must be reined in, subjected to thought experiments that will render them impartial, fair, and respectful of the rights of others, and that they must be induced or forced to acknowledge the dignity of others as well as their duty to universal moral laws, for their inclinations surely would not lead them to these ends. The public sphere is seen as a necessary evil, to discipline unruly passions, and protect rights against aggressors. All of these ideas of justice presuppose that people are in need of disciplining, and yet disciplining has "side-effects"—the twin perils of external and internal tyranny: a disciplining state and a disciplining moralism.

Living under the regime of love changes this entire landscape. First, and most importantly, inclination is no longer the inevitable enemy of fairness or impartiality, but is their ally. When humans love one another, they are not engaged in the project of hurting—of taking away another's dignity, of undervaluing his worth, of violating his rights, of ignoring duties toward him, or breaking promises to him. Secondly, when justice is understood as love, the value of these earlier theories is not displaced thereby, but only shown to fall short. Giving with impartiality is indeed a virtue, but it cannot explain why I would be motivated to give in the first place. Fairness is indeed attractive, but I am not likely even to think of fairness toward another if I do not value him to begin with. The public sphere is not only the creation of legal and economic ties, nor is it solely devoted to reigning in unruly competitiveness. It is also a community formed by bonds of care and such bonds dissolve motives for selfishness, conflict, and war. In this way, justice flows readily from love, as the metaphor in the prophet depicts: "But let justice flow like water, and righteousness like an unfailing stream" (Amos 5:24).[14]

Justice: What's Shakespeare Got to Do With It?

Quite apart from having his own reasons (which we cannot fully know) to make justice a central concern for his plays, we do know that Shakespeare lived at a time when justice was hotly contested in legal thought, when courts of equity and common law courts battled for authority, and when legal codes began to replace earlier codes of honor and revenge.[15] Reformation England had newly achieved access to the Bible, through the wide readership of the Geneva Bible and the King James Bible, and the Protestant emphasis on reading the Bible meant that it was a vital part of culture. As even the Marxist historian Christopher Hill has warned, to understand Reformation England, we ignore the Bible at our peril. In that Christian context, the preoccupation with justice was expressed as the oft-repeated biblical command to love the neighbor. Furthermore, liturgy had been standardized and the Book of Common Prayer was read aloud. Nothing could have seeped deeper into the verbal culture. A brief sample can offer a window onto the way the Book of Common Prayer promulgates the message to love one another, to understand this love as the will of God, and to view love as the perfection of the Law of God. For example, on the first Sunday in Advent, the Book of Common Prayer reads (Rom. 13:8):

Owe we nothing to any man, but this, that ye love one another: For he that loveth another, fulfilleth the Law. For these Commandments, Thou shall not commit adultery, Thou shall not kill, Thou shalt not steal, Thou shall not bear false witness, Thou shalt not lust: and so forth (if there be any other Commandment) it is all comprehended in this saying, namely, Love thy neighbor as thy self. Love hurteth not his neighbor, therefore is love is the fulfilling of the Law.

Calvin's *Sermons on Job* went through five editions in the decade after it was published (1574), was adopted by several parishes for the use of parishioners, and was surely one of Shakespeare's sources.[16] In it, he stresses the centrality of love for the neighbor, and like many others, he interprets that injunction as a warning against over-love of the self.

Let us consider what is imported in this saying, Thou shalt love thy neighbor as thy self. What is the cause that every man steps out of his bounds, and that we love ourselves too much, and despise our neighbors, but because we be not diligent enough in practicing that which is said unto us: namely that we must not be so much given to the love of ourselves, but that we must love our neighbors as ourselves. For we ought to consider, that God hath created us all after his own image, and therewithal that we be all of one nature. Herewith also he tells us, that we ought to agree in true brotherhood with those that are linked unto us.

Luther wrote that "The law of nature is the law of God, and the prophets teach that one person owes love to the other."[17] The deepened centrality of grace meant that an infusion of the value of love is joined to natural law, which is already governed by love:

For when you judge according to love, you will easily decide and adjust matters without any law-books. But when you ignore love and natural law, you will never succeed in pleasing God, though you have devoured all the law-books and the jurists...A good and just decision...must come from a free mind...Such a free decision, however, is given by love and the law of nature, of which the reason is full.[18]

Here, reason is not opposed to love, but in harmony with it. When Reformation theology emphasized the necessity of divine and human love and that flowed into a culture already saturated with a belief that loving relations are part of the fiber of the universe in which human beings participate, a worldview takes hold, one that also inflects the energetic legal and economic debates about justice.[19] Add Shakespeare to the mix and the result is a perfect storm: a drama that often depicts justice as love.[20]

II

The Law of Love

Love worketh no ill to his neighbour: therefore love is the
fulfilling of the law.

ROMANS 13:10 (KING JAMES VERSION)

Teaching a course on Justice in the Law school, I quickly discerned
that our future lawyers did not naively equate the law with justice. They certainly did not anticipate that in upholding the law they
were inevitably upholding justice. After all, in Socrates and Jesus, both
classical philosophy and Christianity have at their center figures condemned by the law but innocent in the eyes of justice. Remarkably
enough, both traditions rest on founding stories of the failure of law to
achieve justice. To be sure, classical and religious views are not univocal: in Aeschylus' final tragedy of the *Oresteia*, *The Eumenides*, Athena
establishes courts of law for the purpose of executing justice, and in the
Bible, Moses appoints judges to carry out justice (Exod. 18:21). Still,
why isn't the law *always* expected to be just? Why isn't its very purpose
conceived as the ensuring of justice? Over time, I began to view the
separation of law and justice as not only disturbing but even dangerous, and this led me to interrogate the assumptions that made that
separation seem inevitable. I began by backing up to a time—a utopian
time—when they were not separated, unearthing a vision of law and
justice as so radically identical that separating them was not yet thinkable. This is the moment I want to linger on here with the hope that

by retrieving it, we can rediscover the resources to rebuild that vital connection between justice and law in our time.

Where was this identity of law and justice to be found? Ironically, in the Hebrew Bible. I say "ironically" because precisely the opposite charge has been made against it, in particular. The rhetoric is familiar: the letter [presumably, the law] kills, but the spirit [presumably justice] lives. According to that charge, the Hebrew Bible is full of empty procedures, legalistic rules, hollow at best, but at worst, even inspiring transgressions of the law by enumerating them. Never mind that this version of the Hebrew Bible was crafted by a medieval supercessionist version of Christianity that was not shared by either Jesus or Paul and that it was fueled by anti-Semitism. It has been remarkably tenacious. Much of Christian theology even saw the law as a stumbling block to justice, as inhibiting the realization of justice.[1] In philosophy, from Plato on, law is regarded as formal while justice is seen as substantive, a view echoed in the political theory that tends to prefer "procedural justice," formal justice, for the project of defining justice substantively is too allusive and too conflicted. In light of this frequent separation of law from justice in both Christian and philosophical thought, the radical identity of the law and justice that characterizes revelation in the Hebrew Bible seems all the more remarkable.

In the Bible, the law is not offered as a legal document: instead and notably, it is embedded in a story. That story tells of the ancient Israelites becoming anxious at the disappearance of Moses when he had gone up the mountain to receive the law from God, and it describes their request to his brother Aaron, in Moses' absence, to "make us a god to go at the head of us" (Exod. 32:1). They take the gold rings from their ears, melt them down and make a golden calf, and then they declare that this is the god who brought them out of Egypt. Meanwhile, Moses has been receiving the law and the first prohibition is "you shall have no other God," followed immediately by the specification that "you shall not make yourself forged images ... you shall not bow down to them or serve them." So, the first command of the Law is against idolatry, but the Law is given in the narrative context of practicing idolatry. In short, the law is broken even as it is given. Hence, the force of the law is executed, in this narrative, on those who are in the very process of receiving it. They are accountable to the law, must answer to the law, even when they are not yet fully under the law.

[Moses] went down from the mountain with the two tablets of the testimony in his hands, tablets that were written on both sides...And the tablets were the work of God, and the writing was the writing of God...And as soon as he came near the camp and saw the calf and the dancing, Moses' anger burned hot, and he threw the tablets out of his hands and broke them at the foot of the mountain.   (Exod. 32:15–19)

It seems that the people are not qualified to receive this law, are not deserving of it, because they are in the very act of transgressing its first tenet. But not qualified according to what? Is it according to a principle of justice that precedes the law, a justice that must be prior to the law and even exceed it? According to that reading, the story would recount how, having violated justice, the people cannot have the law. Justice would be the precondition for receiving the law. But this reading collapses before the most compelling aspect of this narrative: it is precisely the first command of *the law*—the law, and not a prior justice—that they are violating in the narrative, and it is by that infraction of the *law* that they thereby disqualify themselves for it. Worshipping idols, they thereby render themselves unworthy of the law that forbids their worship of idols. Violating justice and breaking the law are apparently not separable here. In this way, the biblical case defies the usual logic that would separate justice from law, the oft-noted importance of reserving a possibility of a justice that would exceed, contradict, or even be indifferent to the Law.

Here the justice so often believed to be beyond the law is also the justice *of* the law. Despite the dominant philosophical tradition that separates justice from law as well as the religious traditions that voice discomfort with the Hebraic law, here, the gift of justice is synonymous with the gift of the law.

The Biblical Love Commands

What is this law that is identical with justice? Again, I will follow the path blazed by the prophets and the rabbis, by Jesus and by those Christian commentators who summarize the law as the "love commands": to love God, to love the neighbor, and to love the stranger. When Jesus was asked what is the greatest of the commandments, he foiled those who wanted to trip him up with his answer: invoking Deut. 6:5, he said, " 'Love the Lord your God with all your heart and with all your soul and with all your mind,' This is the first and greatest commandment. And the second is like it: 'Love your neighbor as yourself.' All the Law and the Prophets hang on these two commandments" (Matt. 22:36–40). And Paul chimes in, "the one who loves another has fulfilled the law...Love does no wrong to a neighbor; therefore, love is the fulfilling of the law" (Rom. 13:8–10). The law is to love, and this achieves justice. This reverberates throughout rabbinic and Christian commentators.[2]

Let us address three aspects of this understanding of justice as love. First, in the commandment to love, what is the meaning of love? Secondly, in the command to love the neighbor, who is the neighbor? And finally, what can it mean to command one to love? How does that seeming oxymoron, the command to love, promote justice?

First, the meaning of love. The Hebrew Bible rarely engages in descriptions of emotional life, so rarely that the instances stand out: God repents having destroyed the earth in the Flood, Jacob loves Rachel, David mourns Absalom, and Jeremiah suffers—a lot. While the command to love may refer to a feeling, its contexts suggest another emphasis: the command to love appears with injunctions about how to *treat* others; love is manifest in action. For example, to love God is to follow his laws and to honor his holiness. It is not thinkable to love God and despise his laws. To love one's fellow is to comprehend his needs and respond to them. In the injunction, "Thou shalt love thy neighbor as thyself" (Lev. 19:18), the referent is not restricted to the Israelites; the stranger is explicitly included among those one is enjoined to love: "the stranger that dwelleth with you shall be unto you as one born among you, and thou shalt love him as thyself; for ye were strangers in the land of Egypt" (Lev. 19:34 KJV). The widow, the orphan, and the stranger are singled out in the account of those to whom we owe this love, and these are not people we would describe as autonomous individuals claiming the right to respect—although they are certainly that—so much as people in need. The model seems to be of humans, not as brutish, self-interested, aggressive, and competitive (the model Hobbes bequeathed), nor as autonomous and choosing their course freely (the Kantian legacy), but as needing: as hungry, dispossessed, lonely, mourning, lacking protection. To be just is to love these people; that is, recognize and provide for their needs.

The Bible suggests that what we do when we love is give. The Hebrew word for "love," *ahavah* has the root, *hava*, of "to give," so that *ahavah* suggests both to love and to give. "It is he who sees justice done for the orphan and the widow, who loves the stranger and gives him food and clothing. Love the stranger then, for you were strangers in the land of Egypt" (Deut. 10:18–19). In this formulation, "to see justice done" is not to measure out some distribution or retribution, but to love, and to love is to give to the stranger, that is, to recognize and to answer the needs of the stranger because you were once a stranger and your vulnerability teaches love for the vulnerable. This love issues in concrete action: "You are neither to strip your vine bare nor to collect the fruit that has fallen in your vineyard. You must leave them for the poor and stranger" (Lev. 19.10). According to Lenn Goodman, the Jewish tradition sees giving as an obligation. This, then, is how it understands justice. Such justice is "no mere matter of convention nor a product of some agreement;" indeed, "Justice is not a contract at all."[3] This obliga-tion, to give, is incumbent upon all of us: it is not dependent upon the presence of any particular virtue in the person, nor is it specifically a response to another's claim, or "right," that we recognize their dignity.[4] It certainly includes that minimally, but demands more: the obligation to give is primarily our response to another's need. The stranger and the poor are presumed to need the fruit of my vineyard; hence, it is just that I leave some for them (Lev. 19:10). Remarkably enough, at the beginning of the Exodus narrative, God describes his own love of the people as a response to his perception of their need: "I have seen the miserable state of my people in Egypt, I have heard their appeal to be rid of their slave-drivers. Yes, I am well aware of their sufferings. I mean to deliver them . . ." (Exod. 3:7–8). The simplicity of the parallel verbs is striking: because he has *seen* and *heard* their suffering, he means to *deliver* them. Is this justice, love, or both, impossible to separate?

The understanding of love and justice as *giving* is also evident in God's relation to the Israelites in the wilderness when the heavens rain food for the hungry wanderers: "Now I will rain bread down from the heavens" (Exod. 16:4). But this abundant gift is also the occasion for a lesson. Hoarding makes no sense in an economy where justice is love and love is giving. It clogs the system. When the ancient Israelites make the mistake of hoarding, God punishes them, rotting their bread, to teach the divine distribution of resources. "This is Yahweh's command: Everyone must gather enough of it for his needs . . . They gathered it, some more, and some less. The man who had gathered more had not too much, and the man who gathered less had not too little. . . . Each found he had gathered *what he had needed*" (Exod. 16:16–18, italics added). Divine abundance seems to give way to human distribution, according to need.

And now, the second question, who is the neighbor? A lot of the discourse on that question has been preoccupied with whether the neighbor is one's countrymen, his kin, his religious or ethnic brother, or if the neighbor is a reference to all others, making the command a universal one. The word in Hebrew *re'akha* has been translated more helpfully as fellow, fellowman.[5] How does Leviticus depict this fellowman? First as the poor and as the stranger. Our fellow man is someone who does not have enough, and so we must feed him, and someone who is away from home, and so we are obligated to reach out to such a person. In Leviticus 19, the fellow is also depicted as someone who can be exploited, lied to, robbed, someone whose wages can be withheld, someone who can be slandered, who can be hated, and someone, moreover, from whom that hatred can be hidden instead of having his offense openly explained to him (defining "harm" far more broadly than contemporary liberal rights does). The list also includes someone who cannot speak and someone who cannot see. In short, one's fellow human is not figured here as a fortress of strength, self-sufficiency, or autonomy—the modern imaginary subject whose right to freedom must be protected. No, the fellow human, from the poor to the stranger, from one who offends unknowingly to one who engages with naïve trust in unfair transactions, from the speechless to the blind, is the very portrait of vulnerability. What then does it mean to love such a fellowman? To respect him, indeed, but far more: to help him.

I want to pause now over the command itself to love, rather than the object of that love. "A command to love" sounds jarring. Commands, after all, suggest requirements, obligations, duties. Love, in contrast, suggests precisely a response that cannot be required, an inclination instead of a duty. If the gulf between justice and law is wide in most of western thought, the distance between duty and love is a veritable canyon. As we have seen, duties, obligations, and commands are understood as the province of reason. Love is understood to be in the province of feeling, and in varying ways in a host of thinkers, that emotion must be subdued by reason. For Kant, the moral act follows the dictates of duty, and not inclination.

For love as an inclination cannot be commanded; but beneficence from duty, when no inclination impels us and even when a natural and unconquerable aversion opposes such beneficence, is practical, and not pathological love. Such love resides in the will and not in propensities of feeling, in principles of action and not in tender sympathy; and only this practical love can be commanded.[6]

So, what can this bizarre (if familiar) formulation, "a command to love," mean? For the philosopher Emmanuel Levinas, to obey love is to act on our responsibility for the other, to heed that responsibility. Love is to be obeyed, performed, in action. Hence, duty and love are not separable after all.

I readily admit that everyone does not interpret the biblical love command in this way. Freud speaks for one modernist sensibility when he responds,

Let us adopt a naive attitude towards it as if we were hearing it for the first time, and we shall be unable then to suppress a feeling of surprise and bewilderment. Why would we do it? What good will it do us? But, above all . . . How can it be possible? My love is something valuable to me which I ought not to throw away without reflection. It imposes duties on me for whose fulfillment I must be ready to make sacrifices. If I love someone, he must deserve it in some way . . . He deserves it if he is so like me in important ways that I can love *my*self in him; and he deserves it if he is so much more perfect than myself that I can love *my* ideal of my own self in him.[7]

The pronouns "my," "me," or "I" appear eleven times in that brief passage which is ostensibly about loving another. He goes on to comment on the command to love the stranger:

If he is a stranger to me and if he cannot attract me by any worth of his own or any significance that he may already have acquired for *my* emotional life, it will be hard for me to love him. Indeed, I should be wrong to do so, for my love is valued by all my own people as a sign of my preferring them, and it is an injustice to them if I put a stranger on a par with them. But if I am to love him (with this universal love) merely because he too is an inhabitant of this earth, like an insect, an earth-worm or a grass-snake, then I fear that only a small modicum of my love will fall to his share.

Then, he drops all pretense: "I must honestly confess that he has more claim to my hostility and even my hatred." Is this perversity, this unabashed defense of self-interest at the expense of other-regarding, the consequence of separating eros from agape, and assuming that the subject is governed by his pleasure principle and his death drive, instead of the call of another? Is this the cost of individualism, secularism, even modernism?

But here, what does love have to do with justice? This biblical understanding of justice as loving the fellow, loving the stranger, expressed as giving to the needy, is not the same as our usual understandings of justice, either as fulfilling a contract, duty to the moral law, a calculus of utility, distributing equitably or in just proportion, nor retribution for an injury. Giving to those in need is not quite based on their desert, their merits, nor is it precisely the same as their right. Although attention to the dignity of others is certainly implicit in this love command, one's dignity is not the same as one's vulnerability. What the fellow claims is not his right, his freedom to possess his goods or pursue his ends without interference; what he claims is my responsibility to care for him. That sets the bar high for justice, and it is small wonder that people fear it and call it by nasty names like paternalism. Much easier to just let people alone than to care for them. No wonder that political thought has balked at this onerous demand.

Two of the common models that govern justice thinking seem to be opposed. In one, people must be treated according to their desert: so the best pianist should win the scholarship to the conservatory. Anything else would be unjust. In another, all people are equally deserving so the role of justice is to equalize. Everyone should go to the conservatory. Efforts to reconcile them abound: one version says all need equal opportunity but then, may be rewarded unequally, in another version, all humans are deserving because all are God's creatures, or in secular terms, all are endowed with an inherent dignity that should not be violated. Another version suggests that there are baseline rights everyone deserves (not to be abused) and that on top of that, rewards are meted out according to greater deserts.[8] But all of these elaborate efforts to reconcile contradictory intuitions about justice are needed when justice concerns evaluating the "worth" of the object. When justice is focused on the giving itself, and is understood as the response to another's need, the concern about deserts and equalities withers. The giving mother is not likely to puzzle over whether both infants are deserving of equal milk. Rather, she is responding to perceived need.

Justice as love, love expressed as giving, humans as full of needs. All that I have delineated is a very different portrait of justice in the

Hebrew Bible from the one common in cultural currency which imagines a God of wrath poised to punish transgressors, one whose terrible curses far outnumber his blessings, whose talk of violence against his people—of their starvation and exile, leaving only a remnant surviving—informs the historical narrative spanning Deuteronomy to 2 Kings and fills the poetry of the prophets. This understanding of justice also seems to be a far cry from the religious intolerance I grappled with in the *Curse of Cain*, the one invoked so often to authorize the slaughter of enemies. The portraits of divine wrath are there, and it seems incumbent upon us to reconcile them with the love commands. As we have seen, even as the law is given that forbids killing, the lawgiver goes on a rampage.

To continue the narrative of the broken tablets and the broken laws:

Moses stood in the gate of the camp and said, "Who is on the Lord's side? Come to me." And all the sons of Levi gathered themselves together to him. And he said to them, "Thus says the Lord God of Israel, 'Put every man his sword on his side, and go to and fro from gate to gate throughout the camp and slay every man his brother, and every man his companion, and every man his neighbor.'" And the sons of Levi did according to the word of Moses; and there fell of the people that day about three thousand men. And Moses said, "Today you have ordained yourselves for the service of the Lord, each one at the cost of his son and of his brother, that he may bestow a blessing upon you this day." (Exod. 32:15–29)

Where is the God of love in this scene? How do we understand this seeming contradiction? Is this God a dictator who will not tolerate a threat to his regime? Is this intolerance to other gods an intolerance toward other notions of the good? What is this obsession with "idolatry" that makes it the motive for all kinds of terror? Biblical justice is not easy. It comprehends both a commandment to love the other, including the stranger, and to wipe out the idolater. I daresay it is easier to swallow the first, especially in light of our association of intolerance with terror. But we are being challenged to understand this loving God as offering a gift of justice, and he only destroys those who refuse that gift. But how do we account for the violence of this enforcement? That is, what is so intolerable about idolatry? Indeed, the rabbinic tradition, in an effort to explain the severity of this punishment, surmised that the Hebrews had been given the law against idolatry, disobeyed, *been asked to repent and refused*, so that they were punished for being stiff-necked. But the scene may require less interpolating to be explicable, for idolatry is not only given primacy of place in the list of commands, but it also is persistently depicted as anathema in the Bible.

The Idolatry of Injustice

I think it helpful to make a distinction between political idolatry on the one hand and the idolatry of injustice on the other, and beware of the dangers of confusing them.[9] Political idolatry looks like intolerance toward the other simply because he is the Other: what the Other worships is "an idol" and hence, such worshippers are "infidels." This association of foreign gods with idolatry has a political feel; after all, one man's idol is another's God. Undergirded by a logic of exclusivism, of "us against them," and nervousness about defending the borders of identity, this charge of idolatry is often a thin veneer used to justify aggression against the foreigner. During wars of religion, the charge of idolatry is flung around repeatedly. During the Reformation, anything associated with Catholicism, for example, was idolatrous. Historically, charges of idolatry were also used as weapons in the conquest of the new world against Natives, in the English Civil War on both sides, the American Civil War on both sides, in the Spanish Inquisition to expel Jews, in Bosnia during so-called ethnic cleansing, and this rhetoric recurs today.[10] Abraham Lincoln said in his Second Inaugural Address that "Both sides read the same Bible, both pray to the same God and each invokes his aid against the other." The biblical prophets repeatedly figure idolatry as the *foreign* wife's betrayal of her husband. The marriage of Israel and God is betrayed by the adulterous Israel and the metaphor that appears at the opening of the book of Hosea—"Go marry a whore. And get children with a whore; for the country itself has become nothing but a whore by abandoning YHVH" (1:2)—is so shocking to the rabbis that Maimonides and Ibn Ezra consider the entire story as a visionary dream. (One Midrash changes the whore image to a wife "looking disreputable, her house untidy, the beds not made.") The political aspect comes into view when the terms idolater, pagan, barbarian, and infidel are used, often interchangeably, to denigrate the foreigner. "Other gods" can be regarded as threatening because the option of multiple notions of the Good threatens the coherence of the community.

And what of the idolatry of injustice? This verges on being a contradiction from the first sense with its ideological emphasis on foreign
gods, on idolatry as adultery, on the dangers of the foreign woman
who lures the Israelite into her idolatrous practices and beliefs. This
second sense is also biblical, but it has had a long theological and
philosophical career: idolatry as nothingness, as void, as vanity. In
Jeremiah, God complains, "For my people have committed two evils;
they have forsaken me, the fountain of living waters, and hewed
them out cisterns, broken cisterns, that can hold no water." The idol
as broken cistern. Isaiah also associates idols with nothing: "They that
make a graven image are all of them vanity; and their delectable
things shall not profit; and they are their own witnesses; they see not,
nor know; that they may be ashamed" (44:9). By Paul this association
of nothingness with idols had grown strong. "So then, we know that
an idol is nothing at all in the world and that there is no God but
one" (1 Cor. 8:4–6). To worship nothingness is to be attached to illu-
sion, to falsehood.

In this understanding of idolatry, the question is not religious
pluralism, the lure of the foreigner, so much as misguided thinking—
although they do often overlap. This sense of falsehood deepens into
error, and much of the concern with *representation* in idolatry concerns
error—the venerator is conceived as falling into the error of mistaking
the object, the icon, for the God. In the course of Christian thought,
this sense of error deepens into sin. Idolatry is a symptom of the power
and success of the Antichrist. In his short but important treatise, "On
Idolatry," Tertullian describes the sin of idolatry as so comprehensive
that it includes virtually all other sins: the idolater is a murderer, forni-
cator, adulterer, committer of fraud and contumely; in sum, "idolatry
savours of opposition to God."[11] Augustine expands idolatry to all
desire that eclipses the rational tendencies of the soul: "In worshipping
idols, men are in reality worshipping demons" who seduce them, lure
them into an infection of the will. Nachmonides cites Deut. 32:17,
saying "Scripture ridicules them, saying they sacrifice to demons who
are no gods at all." Under the reign of universal justice, "other gods"
signal, not the god of foreigners, so much as attachment to error, and
as such, a threat to justice itself.

In contrast to the exclusivism that is the hallmark of political
idolatry, the "idolatry of error" is not attached to one's political enemies, but to the enemies of justice itself. When justice is the real

thing, presumably it does not know exceptions. This is not the false universalism that excludes any outside of its purview—the logic that "all men are brothers" which reduces the non-brother to inhuman, as the US did in its racial legislation against Blacks and the Nazis did against Jews—not the intolerance of a people against foreigners, nor of a ruling class toward the dispossessed—but universal intolerance of injustice itself.

There is danger here—the danger is when we mistake one for another: when we destroy so-called idolaters in the name of universal justice when we are in fact only intolerant of difference, or conversely, when we condone "as difference" what is in reality unjust. The difficulty of ethical life is precisely discerning this difference. The opportunities for hypocrisy are rife, well-noted by Nietzsche, "Now I can really hear what they have been saying all along: 'We good men—we are the just'—what they desire they call not retaliation, but 'the triumph of justice'; what they hate is not their enemy, no! they hate 'injustice,' they hate 'godlessness.'"[12]

The biblical version of justice, then, is not that it is culturally specific, or multiple, subject to negotiation, nor that it is the contingent justice of the ruling party. It is far less fashionable. Casting it as a revelation from God makes justice absolute, transcendent, and universal. That is, the biblical narrative offers justice, not as opinion (and hence, subject to debate and discussion as Plato depicts it), but as divinely given, uncompromising truth (although what this is will be endlessly debated in rabbinic and priestly commentaries). This truth is represented as life-altering and world-changing. To stray from it—to worship idols— is to be lost in error, devoted to wrongdoing.

The contemporary philosopher Alain Badiou is helpful here, when he describes a "truth event" as breaking disruptively, unpredictably, into the familiar world in all of its irreducible, incommunicable singularity, beyond all conventional understanding. He adds that ethics is not just that singular revelation of truth, but an ongoing process, and the process of remaining faithful to that truth constitutes the subject. While he has had no difficulty associating the truth-event with the advent of Christ—Badiou pursues the analysis in his book on St Paul where, as one New Testament scholar has put it, Paul is virtually a Maoist—he is notably less interested in the radical revelation that marks the Sinai event. And yet this revelation exemplifies his understanding beautifully: the narrative describes the creation of subjects who are asked to be faithful to the event—and it gives dire warnings against pseudo-events, fake truths, and false idols. I hardly need to rehearse the aura of the exceptional that fills the narrative of the Sinai revelation, the radical break from the ordinary, from life as they knew it, with Moses leading them, not only out of Egypt, out of their habitual slavery, but also out of their camp in the wilderness to suddenly encounter a terrifying sound and light show:

now at daybreak on the third day there were peals of thunder on the mountain and lightning flashes, a dense cloud, and a loud trumpet blast, and inside the camp all the people trembled... The mountain of Sinai was entirely wrapped in smoke, because God had descended on it in the form of fire. Like smoke from a furnace... Louder and Louder grew the sound of the trumpet. Moses spoke, and God answered him with peals of thunder.   (Exod. 19:16–19, The Jerusalem Bible)

The Truth that is delivered here has no place in the prior situation. Under the terms that reigned prior to revelation, it would be unnameable, unintelligible. The demarcation of the place of the event also points clearly to its break with the prior setting: "God said to Moses, 'Go down and warn this people not to pass beyond their bounds to come and look on God, or many of them will lose their lives... Mark out the limits of the mountain and declare it sacred'" (Exod. 19:21–4). In the philosopher's language: "A truth punches a 'hole' in knowledges, it is heterogeneous to them, but it is also the sole known source of new knowledges."[13]

The atmosphere at Sinai trembles with something else besides the shock of newness—with threat, even with violence. The people tremble before this God, begging Moses to intercede lest they die (Exod. 20:19). The face of Moses is radiant from his encounter with God, and he must veil himself for others even to be able to withstand the sight of him. Only before God and before the elders, to whom he communicates this startling justice, is he unveiled. It seems that not only the message, but also the messenger is unbearable. The revelation of the law is felt as a crisis: with the entry of this demand for justice, the world changes decisively.

Furthermore, because the subject who is created by this event— the new person—did not exist under the horizon of justice prior to it, that justice commands the hearer to a terrifying moment of decisiveness: will he accept this call to justice? The first answer is univocal and affirmative: when Moses relates the words of God to the people "all the people said with one voice, 'All that he has spoken we will do; we will obey' " (Exod. 24:3, 7). In his comments on the revelation, Levinas has pointed out that "The term evoking obedience here ['we will do'] is anterior to that which expresses understanding ['we will listen'] and in the eyes of the Talmudic scholars is taken to be the supreme merit of Israel, the 'wisdom of an angel.'... This obedience before understanding is against Kantian logic, for this biblical ethic cannot be reduced to a categorical imperative in which a universality is suddenly able to direct a will. It is an obedience, rather, which can be traced back to the love of one's neighbor...a love that is obeyed, that is, the responsibility for one's neighbor."[14] The demand of Revelation, then, is not a list of rational commands—rather it is a "love that is obeyed."

The difficulty of being faithful to the event—of being just— preoccupies the biblical narrative during and after the revelation. In this sense, the Revelation is indeed understood as a process, the process of struggling to remain faithful to the truth of the revelation. The wrong paths soon beckon. According to Badiou, there are three ways to betray the truth event: disavowal, trying to follow old patterns as if nothing had happened; false imitation of the event of truth; and a direct "ontologization" of the event of truth, that is, its reduction to a new positive order of being. The Exodus narrative depicts the ancient Israelites betraying the revelation in every sense. They doubt the validity of the event, murmuring "Is Yahweh with us or not?" (Exod. 17:7), disbelieving: "you have brought us to this wilderness [not to emanci- pate us] but to starve this whole company to death!" (Exod. 16:3). They give their allegiance to a pseudo-truth, and they interpret their eman- cipation as due to an idol of gold: "They have been quick to leave the way I marked out for them; they have made themselves a calf of molten metal and worshipped it, 'Here is your God, Israel,' they have cried, 'who brought you up from the land of Egypt!' " (Exod. 32:8–9). Here, the danger of idolatry, injustice, enslavement, and evil are one: as Aaron laments, "you know how prone these people are to evil" (Exod. 32:23). The revelation is betrayed. And for justice to reign, the erring commu- nity must be corrected, however brutally. The law must be enforced— and we learn, thereby, about the force that inheres in law. It can be broken, but it can not really be refused. Once the Law of Justice is given, there is no way to be outside of this Law, for divine revelation is world-altering and subject-altering.

In the Exodus narrative, Moses is offered, in contrast to this wide-spread response, as embodying unswerving fidelity and missionary zeal, a true Revolutionary set in relief against the backsliding people. Moses demands fidelity to the revelation, to the truth of love, and only fidelity to that truth and its Law of justice can constitute the future community. Those who refuse become the enemy—not only to God, not only to one another, but also to emancipation: "Gird on your sword, every man of you, and quarter the camp from gate to gate, killing one his brother, another his friends and another his neighbor" (Exod. 32:27). And so the Marxist Badiou need not frame Paul as the first biblical revolutionary; he could have turned to Moses whose priesthood of believers is formed at the cost of brothers and sons (Exod. 32:29). The revelation starts a revolution. Love is not feeble or even peaceful, not a version of agape separated from power. Rather, love is bound to power, as Tillich noted, even as it is bound to justice. Paul, "the love poet" who authored the verses describing the nature of love in 1 Corinthians, summarized this power of love in his Letter to the Romans. Confronting hardship, persecution, famine, or the sword, love makes us more than conquerors: "For I am convinced that neither death, nor life, nor angels, nor rulers, nor things present, nor things to come, nor powers, nor height, nor depth, nor anything else in all creation will be able to separate us from the love of God..." (Rom. 8:38–9).

The Decalogue of Exodus 20 takes pains to establish the authority of the Lawgiver. Out of the ten commandments, the first three are imperatives that guarantee his authority, and the fourth requires a commemoration of his might. It seems that, after all, there is a demand that is prior to the commands that legislate social justice prohibiting lying, theft, and murder: the demand to acknowledge the authority of this commander, this lawgiver. This is not the king, as throughout much of the ancient world; rather, it is God. And the prologue to all of the commandments grounds his authority on justice with stunning simplicity, "I am the Lord your God who brought you out of the land of Egypt, out of the House of slavery. Thou shalt have no other gods before me."[15] This God has released you from the house of slavery to the house of justice. To follow the law is not to be enslaved to this God for freedom consists only in his law. In his discussion of three kinds of knowledge, Levinas describes " 'accepting the law before you know what the law is' as the third option: not the one offered by philosophy, a knowledge you exercise before action, a consideration you gain, with a safe distance, in security, and then having known, acting, nor the second option, of acting in the dark, impulsively, without knowledge, or naively, like a child. The horizon of philosophy offers these two options, one the obverse of the other." Levinas turns to religion to discern a third option, loving the source of the law, accepting the law as a responsibility that will widen into horizons heretofore unknowable. And this option of accepting a potentially infinite responsibility leads him to invoke the Talmudic commentary: it is "as if God were tilting the mountain like a basin on top of the Israelites and telling them, you may either accept my law or I drop the mountain on you."[16]

In this biblical narrative, without obedience to the law, one is enslaved—to falsehood, to error, to wrongdoing. And this danger is specifically described as following another god. As the biblical name for justice is Law; so the biblical name for injustice is Idolatry. This is not an exclusive monotheism of scarce blessings for some and curses for others; instead in this version—the gift of justice—the revelation is for all and can brook no compromise.

The Law of Justice

The effort to universalize the law may surprise some. But the Rabbis (Sanhedrin 56a) reasoned that since Noah is the father of all mankind, the seven commandments given in the Noachide Covenant (Gen. 9:7 ff.) are binding on the whole human race: prohibitions against idolatry, blasphemy, murder, theft, adultery, the eating of animal flesh with blood in it, as well as a positive commandment to set up courts of justice. And Levinas has shown how the pact that began as particular to Israel is opened up until it becomes universal.[17] The pact of Exodus is revisited (among other places) in Deuteronomy 27 and Joshua 7. Deuteronomy describes the recommendations for a ceremony that is to take place upon the Israelites' entry into the Promised Land (after Moses' death). "And on the day you pass over the Jordan...you shall set up large stones, and plaster them with plaster; and you shall write upon them all the words of this law 'very plainly' (ba'er hetev)" (Deut. 27). And then Joshua describes how the law is read to the people of Israel: "and he read all the words of the law, the blessing and the curse, according to all that is written in the book of the law." Indeed, but all of *Israel*:

when the Mishnah deals with this story, it specifies the blessings and
curses that are read: "They turned their faces toward Mt. Gerizim and
began with the blessing: Blessed be the man that maketh not a graven
or molten image. And both these and these answered Amen... And
afterward... they wrote there all the words of the Law in seventy languages, as it is written 'very plainly.'" Levinas notes that what had begun
as a particular, concrete community is now universalized: the law is
written in seventy languages—the law that was broken by some is now
given to all. According to the tradition, the justice that marks the
Hebraic revelation is universal.

That justice is also interior. When the law attains its end, it is inter-
nalized. Then, brother will no longer have to slay his brother:

"The time is coming," declares the Lord, "when I will make a new covenant
with the house of Israel and with the house of Judah. It will not be like the
covenant I made with their forefathers when I took them by the hand to lead
them out of Egypt, because they broke my covenant... This is the covenant
I will make with the house of Israel after that time, declares the Lord, I will
put my law in their minds and write it on their hearts. I will be their God, and
they will be my people. No longer will a man teach his neighbor or a man his
brother, saying, 'Know the Lord,' because they will all know me, from the least
of them to the greatest." (Jer. 31:31)

The love of God and the love of others will no longer need to be
commanded. In Deuteronomy, this is spoken of as "circumcision of
the heart."[18]

What does God ask of you? the text inquires simply. And its answer
describes a God who is just and who gave man justice in his Law: "To
love him, and to serve him by following the laws that for your good
I lay down for you today... Circumcise your heart then and be obsti-
nate no longer, for your god is God of gods... never partial, never to
be bribed" (Deut. 10:12–18). This notion of the just lawgiver as never
subject to bribes, as incorruptible (and these are the kinds of judges
Moses strives to appoint in Exod. 18:21) contrasts with the golden calf,
the very image of bribery manifest as idolatry, a god made to order for
human purposes, a god designed to justify our worst desires (including
greed, competition, violence) instead of an impartial god who dictates
the law of love to us.[19]

Much contemporary political theory takes refuge in the notion that
it is law—and not justice—that can offer a true universal. After all,

they say, substantive justice is particular, contingent, culturally specific. Because one person's notion of justice is so different from another's which emerges in another culture, they must adjudicate their differences through law. Thank goodness for law, for procedures, for offering a formal universal. Stuart Hampshire has offered a clear expression of this: "...fairness in procedure is an invariable value, a constant in human nature.... Because there will always be conflicts between conceptions of the good, moral conflicts, both in the soul and in the city, there is everywhere a well-recognized need for procedures of conflict resolution...This is the place of a common rationality of method."[20] As Sandel summarizes, "Kantian liberals...need an account [of rights] that does not depend on any particular conception of the good, that does not presuppose the superiority of one way of life over others. Only a justification neutral among ends could preserve the liberal resolve not to favor any particular ends or to impose on its citizens a preferred way of life. But what sort of justification could this be? How is it possible to affirm certain liberties and rights as fundamental without embracing some version of the good life, without endorsing some ends over others?"[21]

But in Exodus, law is not making the claim of being a universal procedure, a dead letter; rather, law is offered as positive universal justice. Procedure is empty like the idols, the broken cistern. The biblical version of empty procedures is not innocent; it is contrasted to justice. Empty ritual, ritual without justice, is described in the book of Amos where God inveighs against it:

"I hate, I despise your feasts, and I take no delight in your solemn assemblies. Even though you offer me your burnt offerings and cereal offerings, I will not accept them...Take away from me the noise of your sons: to the melody of your harps I will not listen. But let justice roll down like waters, and integrity like an ever-flowing stream." (Amos 5:21–4)

Levinas also offers a radical corrective to the procedural justice embraced by so much political theory. "Justice cannot be reduced to the order it institutes or restores, nor to a system whose rationality commands, without difference, men and gods, revealing itself in human legislation like the structures of space in the theorems of geometricians, a justice that a Montesquieu calls the 'logos of Jupiter,' recuperating religion within this metaphor, but effacing precisely transcendence." And then he makes the strong statement that "Ethics is not simply the corollary of the religious but is, of itself, the element in which religious transcendence receives its original meaning."[22]

In these ways, the Bible makes the effort to distinguish between a false universal and a true one. The first is the demand of obedience to an empty law, to mere ritual devoid of justice, even an instrumental use of the divine to justify aggression against one's enemies. The second is a demand for universal justice that knows no compromise. The hard work must be done, with great caution and deliberation, of distinguishing between a political enemy and the enemies of justice. And only a robust understanding of justice can correct that deadly confusion. Justice does not denigrate the foreigner; it loves him, that is, recognizes and provides for his needs.

If the revelation claims to offer the gift of justice, the Hebrew Bible does not underestimate how difficult this gift is. It portrays humanity as persistently failing to respond to others' needs, and the human history of agony confirms that failure. The narrative also insists that the radical entry of justice into the world is uncompromising. The Law says to love the neighbor but the narrative in which it is embedded suggests that violent action against evil is necessary. Loving justice does not command one to love the moral monster. "Let love be genuine: hate what is evil, hold fast to what is good" (Rom. 12:9). Again, there is nothing feeble about the love command. What the gift of justice does in the Hebrew Bible is present one with the harsh reality that, for better or for worse, only giving to those in need, acts performed by the subject, and only by him, can help to create a just world, and only this can relieve despair.

III

The Power of Love

One of the reasons that love is not on the map of political theories of justice is the assumption that it lacks power. Justice seems to require the apparatus of enforcement. How can love be enforced or better, how can love enforce, effect justice? Force and love seem paradoxical if not anathema. How can the public spheres of the political and the judicial include love? And yet, the power of love was not doubted by earlier regimes. "Elizabeth was fond of saying that she was married to her people, and she assured the Commons 'that, though after my death you may have many stepdames, yet shall you never have a more natural mother than I mean to be unto you all.'"[1] Her discourse on love was fulsome: "And though you [my subjects] have had, and may have, many mightier and wiser princes in this seat, yet you never had, nor shall have any, that will love you better."[2] As not only wife to her country, but mother, "she promises constant, self-sacrificing love and implicitly demands, in return, her subjects' affectionate respect."[3] James I based his love on Christ's: "it is a very fit similitude for a king and his people to be like a husband and wife, for even as Christ, in whose throne I sit... is husband to the Church and the Church is his spouse, so I likewise desire to be your husband and ye should be my spouse; and therefore, as it is the husband's part to cherish his wife, to entreat her kindly, and reconcile himself towards her, and procure her love by all means, so it is my part to do the like to my people."[4] Like Elizabeth, James is not content to be only the spouse of his people, but also their father: "as their naturall father and kindly Master, thinketh his greatest contentment standeth in their prosperitie,

and his greatest suretie in hauing their hearts, subiecting his owne pri-
uate affections and appetites to the weale and standing of his Subiects,
euer thinking the common interesse his chiefest particular [concern]."[5]
This was not just rhetoric. The idea that communities are bound
together by love once had more traction. While it survives in religious
communities, it has dropped out of secular understandings of community. But a valuable tradition has therein been lost. Without love
binding communities, there is no effective check on exploitation and
domination. The law can be corralled into supporting fiscal disparity;
the government can be lobbied into catering to special interests.
Indeed, the term "power" is often equated with impulses to dominate,
but it has another meaning altogether when it is framed by love: it
suggests force, the force to influence, to persuade, to connect, to heal,
to sustain, to forgive, and to create. Power becomes not about con-
trolling others and seizing their resources, but about connecting to
others, creating.

The power of love was not underestimated by Shakespeare, whose
romances depict the moral order righted when love prevails and whose
tragedies often suggest that the dissolution of order accompanies a
loveless world. *Romeo and Juliet* takes up the question of how to love
the enemy, and shows us that this demands re-framing the enemy altogether, seeing them anew. *King Lear* takes up the question of loving
the stranger. Both explore the power of love without minimizing the
strength of such counterforces as hatred, self-interest, and greed.

Love the Stranger: *King Lear*

In *King Lear*, the problem of justice surfaces with urgency. Injustice is
rife. The crimes in the play include parents rejecting their children,
children abusing their parents, a master abusing a servant, a brother
betraying his brother, sisters betraying sisters, wives betraying husbands,
crimes of the old against the young, and of the young against the old.
These violations of family bonds grow into threatening the security of
the entire realm, first with civil strife and then with international war.
A king abdicates his authority, filial duty is abandoned, the welfare of
the commonwealth is scorned, greed and rapaciousness are given free
reign. The results of this human injustice are not confined to the earth;
the cosmos itself threatens to go off course. Chaos is come again.

Indeed, *King Lear* seems to chronicle the violation of every concept of justice that political, philosophical, and ethical thought have served up both before, and uncannily, after Shakespeare. These include justice as distribution, retribution, restoration, and the kind of justice associated with natural law, positive law, the rule of the strong, virtue ethics, the moral sense theory, theory of property, utilitarianism, rights theory, charity, equity, and *ordo amoris*. Certainly Shakespeare heard biblical verses and the Book of Common Prayer read aloud weekly in church. He would have known of common law and natural law debates that were around the courts and in the air.[6] Still, the wide range of concepts of justice that this play expresses is remarkable.[7] Together these strains contribute to the play's own unique vision of justice, but that vision is made available, not through its realization in the play—surely *King Lear* does not portray a just world—but by means of clearing away possible, but inadequate, understandings of justice, until only an implied vision, albeit extremely frail, is left.

In the first scene, King Lear is fashioned as a parody of an Aristotelian judge, one who creates justice by dividing equally, but in fact, Lear is not a judge executing justice. He is the head of the realm giving away his kingdom. He does this in a problematic way: by subjecting to measure precisely that which cannot be measured, love. "Which of you shall we say doth love us most?" The king is not really asking for love, but professions of love, and is well satisfied with his daughters' hyperbolic answers. The daughter who is willing to say she loves him most will receive the choicest morsel. Perversely, professions of love are made commensurate with property. Flattery is the currency used to purchase the kingdom. Once flattery is measured and inheritance is assessed, all of the pieces of the kingdom are no longer equal. In this way, the presupposition that goods can be measured, exchanged in proportion, and that such exchange is the basis of social intercourse, of community, is travestied even in the opening scene.

In his confusion of love with property, Lear not only divests his kingdom, but also his youngest daughter. Even in this scene depicting his petulance, he expresses tenderness towards her: "mend your speech a little less you may mar your fortunes" is spoken as helpful advice to her, and then, when he is wounded, he asks, hurt, "but goes thy heart with this?" "So young, and so untender?" (1.1.107–9). He is clearly troubled to relinquish her to one of her suitors, and in his anxiety before her betrothal to another, Lear demands her reassurance that she loves only him. Cordelia will have none of it. How could her love be measured? This daughter who does genuinely love her father refuses to make a mockery of her love: "Unhappy that I am, I cannot heave my heart into my mouth." Instead of giving Cordelia away, Lear throws her away: "Here I disclaim all my paternal care" (1.1.115). That is, Lear responds with acts of such gross injustice—disinheriting his loyal daughter and banishing his loyal servant—that they will reverberate throughout the play's universe.

In that opening scene, the kind of "justice" that is only synonymous with the will of the ruling power (as it is for Plato's Thrasymachus in *The Republic*) is quickly exposed as unjust. Lear exercises his power with cruelty and irresponsibility, all the while insisting that what he rules is law: "come not between the dragon and his wrath" (1.1.124), he tells his loyal servant Kent as he banishes him.

Much later in the play, a much changed Lear will acknowledge that arbitrary uses of authority corrupt justice. He asks the blinded Gloucester: "Thou hast seen a farmer's dog bark at a beggar?... And the creature run from the cur? There thou might behold the great image of authority: a dog's obeyed in office" (4.6.156–61). We witness such a dog when Cornwall blinds Gloucester; he acknowledges that he does so without the "form of justice" but that his power is such that he does not need it (3.7.25–8). Lear himself will launch a fulsome critique of the injustice meted out by legal systems that are rife with hypocrisy and corruptible by wealth.

> Plate sin with gold
> And the strong lance of justice hurtless breaks.
> Arm it in rags, a pygmy's straw doth pierce it.   (4.6.167–9)

His hearer is the blinded Gloucester. Justice is depicted as blind in the iconographic tradition, to signal impartiality. But here, something more sinister is suggested by blindness: the indistinguishable character of the guilty and the guiltless who can imperceptibly change places.

A man may see how this world goes with no eyes. Look with thine ears: see how yond justice rails upon yond simple thief. Hark, in thine ear: change places; and, handy-dandy, which is the justice, which is the thief?   (4.6.146–50)

He exposes the hypocrisy that infects retributive systems,

> Thou rascal beadle, hold thy bloody hand!
> Why dost thou lash that whore? Strip thy own back,

> Thou hotly lusts to use her in that kind
> For which thou whipp'st her.   (4.6.156–9)

Again, the beaters should be beaten: change places, and who is the judge and who the criminal? This critique of the hypocrisy of institutions of justice rests, as any critique does, on ideals. What, then, does this dark play endorse, even implicitly? When someone condemns flattery and hypocrisy, what do they endorse? Genuine feeling, genuine communication, even truth.

The relation of feeling to justice is taken up in *King Lear* repeatedly and the play does depict feeling, both pain and sympathy, as springboards to acts that are remedial. Feelings are not impotent. Importantly, the play does not opt for empathy, even when it seems to sounds that note. Rowan Williams has recently offered a nuanced discussion of empathy, with the very important caution that when it is sentimentalized into "feeling what the sufferer feels," we are at risk of colonizing, rather than helping him. And he further cautions that seeing such emotional identifications as the panacea for injustice is too easy, first, because if the distance between myself and another could be collapsed, rather than manifesting respect for another, I would be absorbing him; and secondly, because that distance cannot be collapsed.[8] But if we do acknowledge that empathy alone is a crude instrument to achieve justice, we do not want to toss out feeling with it, fellow-feeling, feeling for others. We need to avoid simplistic assertions that empathy solves the problem of evil while retaining feeling in our discourse on justice. Lear tells the blinded Gloucester, "If thou wilt weep my fortunes, take my eyes"—acknowledging at once that Gloucester has no eyes to weep and that Lear's misfortunes require Lear's eyes alone to fully see. The statement is a poetic rendering of Williams's caution about empathy: if you want to weep my life, you would have to take my eyes (have my viewpoint), which you cannot.

Cordelia suffers that her father does, but it is her suffering, not his. He is asleep:

> O my dear father, restoration hang
> Thy medicine on my lips, and let this kiss
> Repair those violent harms that my two sisters
> Have in thy reverence made!   (4.7.26–9)

The language of repair is inseparable from her sympathy. Suffering for her father does not render her helpless. Her love restores: it is medicine on her kissing lips.

We must concede that something we don't call empathy is at work here, but what? Perhaps the "power of love." One of the reasons to prefer the language of love to empathy is that love requires the recognition of the distinctness of the other. Then too, it is an activity: for the theologian Søren Kierkegaard love is an activity which must be practiced in order to exist—you cannot love and do nothing. And as we have seen, love is not so much a feeling as an act in the Bible too. The "love commands" are to issue in concrete action: "You are neither to strip your vine bare nor to collect the fruit that has fallen in your vineyard. You must leave them for the poor and stranger" (Lev. 19.10). As we have seen, in that tradition, to love one's fellow is to comprehend his needs and respond to them, to give. In Leviticus 19:18, "Thou shalt love thy neighbor as thyself," the referent is not restricted to the Israelites; the stranger is explicitly included among those one is enjoined to love: "You shall love the stranger, for you were strangers in the land of Egypt" (Deut. 10:18–19). Sometimes the Bible says love the neighbor and sometimes love the stranger and if we get confused, thinking that the neighbor is a stranger and the stranger is a neighbor, that may be useful, for those we think we know—the neighbor—are in fact ultimately inaccessible, but also, however distant, this stranger is completely vital to our sense of ourselves and our own interiority, and hence, is our neighbor.

When Lear, exposed to misery in the storm, enters the hovel, he is finally able to apprehend the misery of Others:

> In, boy, go first. You houseless poverty—
> Nay, get thee in.
>
> .   .   .   .
>
> [*Kneels*] Poor naked wretches, whereso'er you are,
> That bide the pelting of this pitiless storm,
> How shall your houseless heads and unfed sides,
> Your looped and windowed raggedness, defend you
> From seasons such as these? O, I have ta'en
> Too little care of this!   (3.4.26–33)

With its emphasis on the houseless heads, the unfed sides, the naked wretches, Lear intones the biblical understanding of justice as caring for the vulnerable, giving to those in need. The cure for the rulers who have been blind to injustice is for them to suffer themselves:

> Take physic, pomp,
> Expose thyself to feel what wretches feel,

> That thou mayst shake the superflux to them,
> And show the heavens more just.   (3.4.33–6)

This too is not quite empathy—to experience the homeless's experience—for this is a self-dispossessed king, not a beggar. But Lear does suffer, and his suffering impels his will toward acts of justice: "Expose thyself to feel what wretches feel...that thou mayst shake the superflux to them...." This is Shakespeare's version of gleaning the fields.

This lesson in shaking the superflux, gleaning the fields, is also learned by Gloucester when he suffers. When he could see, he was blind to his wrongdoing toward his loyal son Edgar. But in his blindness, he worries about clothing the naked madman who leads him—the disguised Edgar. As Gloucester stumbles toward what he thinks will be his death at the cliffs of Dover, he gives his purse to this poor guide:

> Here, take this purse, thou whom the heavens' plagues
> Have humbled to all strokes. That I am wretched
> Makes thee the happier. Heavens deal so still!
> Let the superfluous and lust-dieted man
> That slaves your ordinance, that will not see
> Because he does not feel, feel your power quickly;
> So distribution should undo excess,
> And each man have enough. Does thou know Dover?   (4.1.67–74)

Here is a striking juxtaposition of a lesson in political philosophy, in fair distribution, with the simple question, do you know the way to Dover, to my chosen place of death. That proximity lends his philosophy the authority of a last will and testament, the summary of a dying man upon life: gleaning the fields, shaking the superflux, distribution undoing excess. But not cold calculated distribution; rather, the force of love. Those who fail to act justly are those who will not see because they will not feel, says the blind man, feelingly.

We see the force of love at work when, in *King Lear*, Cordelia sees the miserable state of her father, grieves at hearing the news of his mistreatment, and amasses an army. Critics have often noted the striking biblical allusion she makes, "Oh father, it is thy business that I go about," invoking Christ's mission, but again, heeding the context is revealing: her pious statement is surrounded by her description of sending an army into England to restore the kingdom to her father. "Our preparation stands in expectation of them: O father, it is thy business that I go about.... No blown ambition does our arms incite, but love, dear love, and our aged father's right" (4.4.22–8). Love musters an army to protect her father's right. Love seeks justice. And when her army fails, it will not be because love is feeble.

Love prompts actions repeatedly. Edgar describes himself as

> A most poor man, made tame to fortune's blows;
> Who, by the art of known and feeling sorrows,
> Am pregnant to good pity.

But he does not stop with pity, the feeling leads to succor:

> Give me your hand,
> I'll lead you to some biding.⁹   (4.6.217–20)

As Calvin wrote, it is not enough to pity the misery of others, but to show our compassion by doing. Feeling must be joined to action, suffering to succouring: "we must also show this compassion of ours by our doings."¹⁰ As Lear says, "Expose thyself to feel what wretches feel...that thou mayst shake the superflux to them...." Furthermore, our help, our acts of charity, are only genuine if accompanied by compassion. Giving must spring from love, not duty. The biblical tradition could not be farther from the Kantian philosophical one.

> ...when we see any man in adversity, and that he hath need of our help, we should be sorry in our heart, and suffer with him in our own person, and thereby be led to do for him according to the ability that God giveth us. *For it is not enough for us to heal such as have need of our aid, but we must also do it with a hearty love. The word alms importeth as much as mercy. But men think they have done an alms deed, when they neither regard nor esteem the person more than a dog, nor suffer any part of his grief, nor (to be short) have any compassion on him, provided only that they give him somewhat: but (to speak properly) that is no alms at all.*¹¹

In the play, the most arresting image of suffering and succouring occurs when Lear awakens from his madness to find Cordelia: the once-banished daughter now asks for her father's blessing, and the remorseful Lear begs her forgiveness.

> O! Look upon me, Sir,
> And hold your hand in benediction o'er me.
> No, Sir, you must not kneel.   (4.7.58–60)

Lear is as much constituted by Cordelia's forgiveness as Cordelia is by her father's blessing. Understanding this, Lear seizes upon these acts of blessing and forgiveness, poignantly imagining a perpetual kneeling contest in their paradisal prison.

> Come, let's away to prison
> We two alone will sing like birds i'the cage
> When thou dost ask me blessing, I'll kneel down
> And ask of thee forgiveness. So we'll live
> And pray, and sing, and tell old tales...   (5.3.8–12)

As critics have oft noted, Lear must lose all to gain all. In the course of the drama, King Lear loses his kingdom, his power, his worldly effects, his sanity, and his identity, but this is accompanied by a rising action: his growing apprehension of what love really is and his growing capacity to experience it. Illusions give way to truth. When he has the entire realm, he does not have what he thinks he wants—Cordelia's hyperbolic professions of devotion. And when he has lost everything, when he and Cordelia are reduced to the space they occupy chained and imprisoned, he has All:

> And we'll wear out,
> In a wall'd prison, packs and sects of great ones,
> That ebb and flow by the moon.   (5.3.17–19)

In their confinement, Lear has glimpsed eternity. He and his beloved Cordelia will outlive the "great ones"—they are merely packs and sects, after all, whose power is so fleeting. Justice will be reframed under the horizon of love.

Not surprisingly, Lear's brutal renunciation of his own child was replete with the discourse of the stranger.

> Here I disclaim all my paternal care,
> Propinquity and property of blood,
> And as a stranger to my heart and me
> Hold thee from this for ever.   (1.1.114–17)

Then, having thoroughly estranged her, he heaps on more: claiming that he would hold her as the most alien of strangers:

> The barbarous Scythian
> Or he that makes his generation messes
> To gorge his appetite, shall to my bosom
> Be as well neighboured, pitied, and relieved,
> As thou my sometime daughter.   (1.1.117–21)

This echoes, but perversely, the biblical injunction to love the neighbor, love the stranger, to pity and relieve him. And Lear will not grant this even to his daughter. In this way, the play weaves the command to love the stranger—for Cordelia has been strangered—into the core of its plot. Lear must learn to love the stranger or he will never be ethical and never be Lear.

By the end, Lear's reunion with the Cordelia he had once banished is the only restoration of goodness in a world achingly bereft of it. Here power is explicitly reframed—not as the power of domination, not as the winning army, but as the triumph of goodness manifest in her forgiveness, her gift of immeasurable love, not withheld nor scorned, however loveless the world around her is. The ingratitude of Cordelia's sisters has driven Lear to madness—how can what should be freely given be withheld? It is Cordelia's measureless giving that restores his sanity. The triumph of the vision of shared love is resounded with exquisite pathos when Lear and Cordelia are held captive to his other daughters' scheming greed, their grasping having won the day, politically.

CORDELIA We are not the first
  Who with best meaning have incurred the worst.
  For thee, oppressed King, I am cast down;
  Myself could else outfrown false fortune's frown.
  Shall we not see these daughters and these sisters?
KING LEAR No, no, no, no! Come, let's away to prison;
  We two alone will sing like birds i'the cage.
  When thou dost ask me blessing, I'll kneel down,
  and ask of thee forgiveness: so we'll live,
  And pray, and sing, and tell old tales, and laugh
  At gilded butterflies, and hear poor rogues
  Talk of court news; and we'll talk with them too—
  Who loses and who wins, who's in, who's out—
  And take upon's the mystery of things
  As if we were God's spies. And we'll wear out,
  In a wall'd prison, packs and sects of great ones,
  That ebb and flow by the moon. (5.3.3–19)

This triumphant love-world is dramatically interrupted by the brutal reminder of their defeat in the political world. Shakespeare is no easy idealist.

EDMUND [to soldiers] Take them away. (5.3.19)

But does Edmund's loveless world really prevail over the love Cordelia and Lear have achieved? Lear claims the gods themselves worship their sacrifice; it is the ultimate value.

KING LEAR   Upon such sacrifices, my Cordelia,
The gods themselves throw incense. Have I caught thee?
He that parts us shall bring a brand from heaven,
And fire us hence like foxes. Wipe thine eyes;
The good-years shall devour them, flesh and fell,
Ere they shall make us weep! We'll see 'em starved first.
Come.   (5.3.20–6)

Two worlds collide before us in this scene, the one of domination
and finitude ("take them away") and the other of love and the infinite
("so we'll live and pray and sing"). Lear asserts that the value he now
embraces—love—cannot be diminished by even the triumph of enemies.
There is more than a hint that Lear understands prison as a safe retreat
from the terrors of worldly machinations "that ebb and flow by the
moon." While the play is not set in a Christian context, the endorsement
of the biblical tradition that elevates love to the highest good is unmis-
takable. That this is accompanied by sacrifice—of goods, of control, and
finally, of life itself—only underscores the ultimate nature of that value.

At the end, *King Lear* scorns both Aristotle's geometric distribution
and Rawls's arithmetic distribution that presuppose that goods are in
scarce supply and the challenge is to apportion them. With love, given
endlessly from an infinite supply, justice takes a new turn. It cannot be cut
up and given to equalize fair distribution of its bits. It cannot be denied—
despite whatever harm is inflicted—and it cannot be lessened by changes
in fortune or time. The play also scorns Kantian duty with its requirement that feeling be bracketed. Love is the wellspring of healing, of restoration, and even of a frail justice in this play. Surely such love is powerful.

And what about the audience? What is the relation between this
theatrical experience and the world outside? What does the audience
experience? We suffer—when Lear is turned out of doors, when
Gloucester is blinded, when a mad Lear and a blind Gloucester com-
miserate, when the reunited Lear and Cordelia are imprisoned, but
perhaps most, when, after Lear and Cordelia's mutual acknowledgement of their love, she dies. Again, *Lear* is not an explicitly Christian
play; to the contrary, it does not allude to an afterlife of rewards or
punishments, nor does it offer a restoration to a good political order.
At its end, we learn that the world will end:

ALBANY   The weight of this sad time we must obey,
Speak what we feel, not what we ought to say.
The oldest hath borne most: we that are young
Shall never see so much, nor live so long.   (5.3.322–5)

But for all of this bleakness, to ignore the discovery of love that occurs is to distort the drama, even to subvert the driving plot, and surely doing so lessens the pain. For what can more painful than to discover love only to lose it? Such pain is unutterable: "O O O O" is all Lear can cry at his daughter's death before expiring from grief. This is the earlier version. Shakespeare rewrote it to express Lear's misguided hope that his daughter might yet live—"the feather yet stirs"—to make the truth even more insupportable for him. Shakespeare's rewrite of Lear's denial suggests what the eighteenth century audiences will acknowledge: her death is unbearable, so unbearable that for 150 years audiences preferred to see another rewritten happier ending. We may learn much by comparing Cordelia's death to that of Desdemona. The latter's complete innocence is stressed in the scene before her murder where she confesses the inability to even imagine betraying her husband. But in his demented jealousy, Othello fails to rediscover her love while she yet lives. Our response is more horror at the unjust murder than pain at gaining and then losing all that matters.

Like Lear, our suffering moves us from self-absorption toward the plight of others. And to the extent that we sympathize with Lear, we learn to love this seeming monster, this utter stranger. In this sense, tragedy does not only show us our helplessness, but makes us capable, even empowers us. We cannot leave a production of *King Lear* apprehending the same world we did when we entered. We see domination, privilege, abuse of authority and even law with a jaundiced eye and we see those in want as demanding our care. The play re-orients the audience to the supreme value Lear discovers, of authentic love—not self-serving flattery, but self-giving love. Not just our world, we too are changed. Whether inside or outside the theater, one can only live differently when he sees himself and others differently.

Shakespeare's reflections on our obligation to the stranger become explicit in his hand-penned additions to the script of *Sir Thomas More*. In his capacity as Sheriff of London, More addresses a violent mob hostile against foreigners on "Ill May Day" 1517, defending the rights of refugees with such eloquence that his words have reached across the centuries to rebuke the present:

> Grant them removed, and grant that this your noise
> Hath chid down all the majesty of England;
> Imagine that you see the wretched strangers,

Their babes at their backs and their poor luggage,
Plodding to the ports and coasts for transportation,

. . . .

And you in ruff of your opinions clothed;
What had you got? I'll tell you: you had taught
How insolence and strong hand should prevail,
How order should be quelled; and by this pattern
Not one of you should live an aged man,
For other ruffians, as their fancies wrought,
With self same hand, self reasons, and self right,
Would shark on you, and men like ravenous fishes
Would feed on one another.

The haunting image of exiling "wretched strangers, their babes at their backs and their poor luggage plodding to the ports and coasts," searching for a place to go, is, in our time, realized photographically with heart-rending realism. But More does not only prophetically conjure this image of the brutal treatment of others. He knows that if such a code of self-interest prevails—"self same hand, self reasons, and self right"—the victimizers will someday be victimized. If the king were

to banish you, whither would you go?
What country, by the nature of your error,
Should give you harbour? go you to France or Flanders,
To any German province, to Spain or Portugal,
Nay, any where that not adheres to England,
Why, you must needs be strangers: would you be pleased
To find a nation of such barbarous temper,
That, breaking out in hideous violence,
Would not afford you an abode on earth,
Whet their detested knives against your throats,
Spurn you like dogs...
                        what would you think,
To be thus used? this is the strangers case;
And this your mountainish inhumanity.[12]

Ironically itemizing foreign lands that are not English allies, "nay, any where that not adheres to England," More's deeper logic is to break down the very categories of foreigner and native, for we are all potentially displaced, all possibly strangers; he warns the locals, "Why, *you* must needs be strangers" (italics added). "Love the stranger," says the

Bible, "for you were once a stranger in the land of Egypt." Stop abusing the stranger, says Shakespeare, for you too could be a stranger.

Love the Enemy: *Romeo and Juliet*

> For where thou art, there is the world itself,
> And where thou art not, desolation.
>
> SHAKESPEARE, *2 Henry IV*

Love does not always take the form of giving tangible things, of shaking the superflux, of gleaning the fields. Sometimes, what we give when we love is attention, acknowledgement, understanding, and sympathy. The sociologist Niklas Luhmann has defined love as communication: "love is...a code of communication, according to the rules of which one can express, form and simulate feelings, deny them, impute them to others, and be prepared to face up to all the consequences which enacting such communication may bring with it." [13] Genuine communication, not misfiring, not half-heard, not almost but not quite speaking to one another, is rare. In *Romeo and Juliet,* for all of its exquisite lyricism, its extravagant metaphors and thrilling figurative language, hardly anyone communicates successfully. The Nurse's failures are the stuff of comedy, Mercutio's of satire and ultimately tragedy, and the plot is full of missed messages, including the final fatal one from the Friar to Romeo that Juliet is not dead but only sleeps, awaiting to be reunited with him.

The notable exception is Romeo and Juliet. Their communication is instantaneous and complete, so complete that they seem to speak to one another even when they are apart and to speak by death and in death. It is so complete that upon first meeting, they spontaneously compose a sonnet together, the complete form of love poetry. Romeo utters the first quatrain, Juliet responds with the second, together they speak the third, and again, together create the final rhyming couplet that ends in their first kiss.

ROMEO   If I profane with my unworthiest hand
  This holy shrine, the gentle sin is this:
  My lips, two blushing pilgrims, ready stand
  To smooth that rough touch with a tender kiss.

JULIET   Good pilgrim, you do wrong your hand too much,
  Which mannerly devotion shows in this;
  For saints have hands that pilgrims' hands do touch,
  And palm to palm is holy palmers' kiss.
ROMEO   Have not saints lips, and holy palmers too?
JULIET   Ay, pilgrim, lips that they must use in prayer.
ROMEO   O, then, dear saint, let lips do what hands do;
  They pray, grant thou, lest faith turn to despair.
JULIET   Saints do not move, though grant for prayers' sake.
ROMEO   Then move not, while my prayer's effect I take.   (1.5.92–105)

All of this imagery of holiness, including Romeo's pilgrimage to a saint and that saint granting his prayer and offering grace, will frame their love from beginning to end. During their courtship, Romeo will speak of Juliet as a bright angel, and at the end, he will be a pilgrim again, but to her tomb where, as at a festive marriage banquet, he will be granted his wish of a kiss and their death bed will become their final marriage bed. Unlike *Lear*, this play more than hints that those deaths are enfolded in a beatitude of eternal love.[14]

But can this religion of love also be passionate? Are we not to distinguish eros from agape? Is their love obsessed with desire rather than the political project of loving the neighbor? Is there not a strong distinction between neighbor love, agape, and passionate love, eros? Will the lovers be so absorbed in their own world that they leave behind corrupted society, indulging in an ecstatic love unto death? Indeed, the lovers become progressively isolated, even from their confidantes who cannot comfort the persecuted lovers. Juliet must separate from her Nurse—"Go counsellor, | Thou and my bosom henceforth shall be twain" (4.1.240–1)—and Romeo must tell the Friar to "talk no more" of philosophy to him (3.3.60). Romeo becomes world-weary as he flies to the side of Juliet in her tomb, telling the apothecary that gold does more murder in this loathsome world than the forbidden poisons he sells. By then, Romeo has left behind the Petrarchan lover's conventions: wounded by desire, losing his self, with language punctuated by deep sighs, a rush of opposing images, heavy lightness. Chastened by Juliet's instructions that he speak "faithfully," instead, Romeo has come to experience a devotion without guile and without measure. Many a reader (and director) has reduced Romeo and Juliet to a private passionate love affair. Many would concur that "Their love is reckless, tending to destruction but it is glorious."[15]

The distinction between eros and agape, love of desire and neighbor love, is the legacy of Anders Nygren, and has been strongly repudiated by many historians of Christian thought. For most of the Middle Ages, love was understood to be theologically on a continuum with cosmic love, with the love that holds all beings together in concord. "The power of love holds together the universe, which is constantly threatening to get out of order. It brings about universal and social harmony, reconciling the elements which would otherwise be at war with each other, and doing the same for men."[16] Sexual passionate love was understood as another "manifestation of the all-pervading love of God, through which the universe was governed."[17] And through sexuality, "the creatures would be participating or cooperating in the creative or generative activity of the Eternal Being, that activity in which... his 'goodness' and his 'love' were believed to lie."[18]

Sexuality was brought to the fore in early modern discussions about "holy matrimony." While the marriage rite itself was contested—was marriage a sacrament or not?—the question of the sanctity of sex itself can be traced to debates about clerical marriage. Reformers understood married sex as devotional. The English bishop John Jewel, in his *Treatise of the Sacraments* (late 1550s), critiqued the position that married sex was somehow polluted: "What are they that call marriage uncleanness, filthiness, a work of the flesh?... That say it defileth a man; and therefore God's ministers may not be married?"[19] His defense of priestly sex is based on his understanding of sex as an act of devotion.

Attending this emphasis on the sanctity of married sex was a renewed abhorrence of sex outside of marriage. "Of Whoredom and Uncleanness," an Edwardian homily, was also quoted in Catholic versions under Queen Mary. Despite the complexity of changing sixteenth-century marriage laws, in the play, Romeo and Juliet have steered a safe course with all the elements of holy matrimony in place: mutual consent, solemnization in church, and consummation in bed. They do all of this in a day and a night and all in secret. Indeed, "the play concerns a civilly disobedient couple who perform a liturgically correct marriage."[20] Theirs is not a secular marriage, but a "holy bond of love." That imagery attending their first encounter of a pilgrim visiting a saint's shrine and receiving grace is deepened when they marry and the "holy church incorporates two in one," a union Friar Lawrence hopes will "turn your households' rancor to pure love." Their sexual devotion together is too brief: Juliet hopefully claims at dawn that "it was the nightingale and not the lark | That pierced the fearful hollow of thine ear," but it is replete with the imagery of fecundity that assures that the created order will continue. Juliet imagines the notes of the nightingale who "sings on yond pomegranate tree," ancient symbol of fertility from the Song of Songs, and in the tradition in visual arts, the hollow of Mary's ear was impregnated with Christ. But Juliet's reverie about their sexual union is tragically broken for Romeo must flee: "It was the lark, the herald of the morn. | No nightingale."

As *King Lear* stages the injunction to love the stranger, with Lear painfully learning to love his estranged daughter and the audience learning to love the stranger Lear, so *Romeo and Juliet* dramatizes the impossible command to love the enemy, its cost as well as its efficacy. How can one love the enemy? Juliet instantly apprehends how. To divest him of whatever effects make him that enemy, the signs attached to him that provoke intolerance, hatred, prejudice. These must be removed, peeled away, in order to reveal the person himself. And the sign that is most laden with hatred is the communal name: Montague, Capulet, Jets, Sharks, Protestant, Catholic. This sign—and as Juliet apprehends it, it is only a sign, a name—clouds our vision of the unique person, making him only symbolic of the enemy. It has no substance, no essence, is neither foot nor face.

JULIET 'Tis but thy name that is my enemy,
Thou art thyself, though not a Montague.
What's Montague? It is nor hand nor foot,
Nor arm nor face nor any other part
Belonging to a man. O, be some other name!
What's in a name?

. . . .

Romeo, doff thy name,
And for that name which is no part of thee,
Take all myself. (2.2.38–49)

Juliet solves the problem of their ancient enmity for herself by stripping Romeo of his hated superficial identity, the "name" (a term intoned repeatedly, six times in this brief speech), and giving all of herself to him instead. Love thy enemy could not be more succinctly dramatized.

Romeo overhears, understands her solution, and eagerly shares it. Newly baptized as Love, he gives up the name of Romeo, willingly shedding his loathed identity marker.

ROMEO   I take thee at thy word.
   Call me but love, and I'll be new baptized.
   Henceforth I never will be Romeo.   (2.2.49–51)

Juliet began her reverie in the night by repeating the troubling name, asking why he has to have it, and then seizing on the solution: Romeo should refuse his name. But if he cannot, she searches for a deeper solution; she is willing to give up her own social identity and renounce her hated family label.

JULIET   O Romeo, Romeo, wherefore art thou Romeo?
   Deny thy father and refuse thy name,
   Or, if thou wilt not, be but sworn my love,
   And I'll no longer be a Capulet.   (2.2.33–6)

Henceforth, for the lovers, Montagues or Capulets are no longer Montagues or Capulets. They are newly baptized, as persons, as lovers (is the play suggesting that full personhood is only achieved in love?). Their love knows no caution, no suspicion, no cynicism, no reservation. Their love, pure, passionate, and potent, overcomes the myriad social injuries and hatreds they face. But not so fast.

First, their love must withstand assaults engendered by others' rage: Tybalt attacking Mercutio, stabbing him under Romeo's arm, Romeo's initial efforts to extend love to Tybalt giving way to vengeance for the death of his friend, the fury of the law as Romeo is banished by the angry Prince, paternal tyranny as Juliet's father demands her marriage to Paris, the misfortune of Friar Lawrence's message not reaching Romeo to inform him that Juliet only sleeps. The obstacles to their sudden love continuing are formidable, but its strength does not waver before any of them.

The first test comes when Romeo kills Juliet's cousin.

JULIET   O God, did Romeo's hand shed Tybalt's blood?
NURSE   It did, it did; alas the day, it did.
JULIET   O serpent heart hid with a flowering face!
   Did ever dragon keep so fair a cave?
   Beautiful tyrant, fiend angelical,
   Dove-feathered raven! wolvish-ravening lamb!

      .   .   .   .

   O that deceit should dwell
   In such a gorgeous palace.   (3.2.71–85)

In her emotional confusion, receiving hateful news about one she loves, Juliet's first response is to indulge in Petrarchan conceits of contraries, "Beautiful tyrant," etc. But when the Nurse condemns Romeo, Juliet's loyalty is awakened.

NURSE   There's no trust,
   No faith, no honesty in men—all perjured,
   All forsworn, all naught, all dissemblers.
     .   .   .   .
   Shame come to Romeo!
JULIET   Blistered be thy tongue
   For such a wish! he was not born to shame;
   Upon his brow shame is ashamed to sit
   For 'tis a throne where honour may be crowned
   Sole monarch of the universal earth.
   O, what a beast was I to chide at him!
NURSE   Will you speak well of him that killed your cousin?
JULIET   Shall I speak ill of him that is my husband?
   Ah, poor my lord, what tongue shall smooth thy name,
   When I, thy three-hours wife, have mangled it?   (3.2.85–99)

Juliet's struggle of loyalties is short-lived: she now casts her lot with her husband. His "name" is no longer hated, but must be "smoothed," restored to the dignity a loving wife gives it.

   Her forgiveness is as sudden and complete as her initial love—a forgiveness that neither the Capulets nor the Prince will share. It is motivated only by love: she knows nothing of the details of the murder of her cousin, only the context of an ancient and ongoing family hatred. And now, having embraced their newly forged bond, she must come to some understanding of his deed. Loving him, she concludes, with no evidence, that the murder must have been self-defense.

       But, wherefore, villain, didst thou kill my cousin?
       That villain cousin would have killed my husband:
       Back, foolish tears, back to your native spring,
       Your tributary drops belong to woe
       Which you, mistaking, offer up to joy.
       My husband lives, that Tybalt would have slain,
       And Tybalt's dead that would have slain my husband.
       All this is comfort. Wherefore weep I then?   (3.2.100–7)

To love the enemy is first, to uncouple him from his hated name, and next, to forgive him for his heinous deeds. We shall learn more of such taxing love. The next obstacle to their love is formidable: the state's decree of Romeo's banishment. How will their love survive that?

> Some word there was, worser than Tybalt's death,
> That murdered me. I would forget it fain,
> But, O, it presses to my memory
> Like damned guilty deeds to sinners' minds.
> Tybalt is dead, and Romeo—banished;
> That 'banished,' that one word 'banished'
> Hath slain ten thousand Tybalts.
> . . . .
> 'Romeo is banished,'—to speak that word,
> Is father, mother, Tybalt, Romeo, Juliet,
> All slain, all dead. 'Romeo is banished!'—
> There is no end, no limit, measure, bound,
> In that word's death; no words can that woe sound.   (3.2.108–26)

In her discourse on "banished"—and the word is intoned five times here—Juliet speaks of endless grief. This parallels her earlier description of her infinite love:

> My bounty is as boundless as the sea,
> My love as deep; the more I give to thee,
> The more I have, for both are infinite.   (2.2.133–5)

Now her infinite love yields infinite pain. "Romeo banished" equals losing her father and mother, Tybalt, Romeo and Juliet. Without him, her entire world ends, "all slain, all dead." Never does the possibility that she could take up life without him arise. There is no such life.

Within three hours of her marriage, Juliet learns her husband has murdered her cousin and is banished: she infers that this has made the consummation of her marriage impossible, and tells her Nurse to take away the cords (the ladder) that lead to her bedroom.

JULIET   Take up those cords. Poor ropes, you are beguiled,
> Both you and I; for Romeo is exiled.
> He made you for a highway to my bed;
> But I, a maid, die maiden-widowed.
> Come, cords, come, Nurse, I'll to my wedding bed
> And death, not Romeo, take my maidenhead.   (3.2.132–7)

This is not hyperbolic melancholy; it is devotion. Without her Romeo, Juliet cannot forge a life. We hear her only imagining death. When he learns of his banishment, his words echo hers. Unable to speak to one another, nonetheless, they communicate, their language very much in accord:

FRIAR LAURENCE   Hence from Verona art thou banished.
   Be patient, for the world is broad and wide.
ROMEO   There is no world without Verona walls
   But purgatory, torture, hell itself.
   Hence banished is banish'd from the world,
   And world's exile is death; then 'banished'
   Is death misterm'd. Calling death 'banished,'
   Thou cutt'st my head off with a golden axe
   And smilest upon the stroke that murders me.   (3.3.15–23)

Intoning the dread word of banished as Juliet does, allowing its significance to reverberate unto death, Romeo, like Juliet, feels the loss of his entire world in losing her. A life without Juliet is unimaginable to him, no life at all.

ROMEO   And sayest thou yet that exile is not death?
   Hadst thou no poison mixed, no sharp-ground knife,
   No sudden mean of death, though ne'er so mean,
   But 'banished' to kill me?—Banished!
   O Friar, the damned use that word in hell;
   Howlings attend it. How hast thou the heart,
   Being a divine, a ghostly confessor,
   A sin-absolver, and my friend professed,
   To mangle me with that word 'banished'?
FRIAR LAURENCE   Thou fond mad man, hear me but speak a word.
ROMEO   O, thou wilt speak again of banishment.   (3.3.43–53)

The Friar offers Romeo no effective comfort. Communication fails between the Friar and Romeo, even as it succeeds with Juliet.

FRIAR LAURENCE   I'll give thee armour to keep off that word,
   Adversity's sweet milk, philosophy,
   To comfort thee, though thou art banished.
ROMEO   Yet banished? Hang up philosophy!
   Unless philosophy can make a Juliet,
   Displant a town, reverse a prince's doom,
   It helps not, it prevails not. Talk no more.   (3.3.54–60)

In contrast to love, philosophy is targeted here as utterly impotent: it cannot reverse a Prince's verdict, it cannot restore Juliet to Romeo.

   As dire as that verdict of banishment is, the young lovers face yet a new horror. The parents Juliet seeks for comfort heap on her an impossible demand: not only that she live without Romeo, but with another husband, unwittingly insisting on turning the faithful lover into an adulteress. Juliet's marriage bed with Romeo has only concluded—he has just left at the window—when her mother arrives to announce her planned imminent marriage to another. In the double entendres that ensue, Juliet speaks of her devotion to Romeo while her typically uncomprehending mother gleans another meaning altogether.

CAPULET'S WIFE   Well, girl, thou weep'st not so much for his [Tybalt's] death,
    As that the villain lives which slaughtered him.
JULIET   What villain, madam?
CAPULET'S WIFE   That same villain Romeo.
JULIET [aside]   Villain and he be many miles asunder.—
    God pardon him! I do, with all my heart;
    And yet no man like he doth grieve my heart.
CAPULET'S WIFE   That is because the traitor murderer lives.
JULIET   Ay, madam, from the reach of these my hands:
    Would none but I might venge my cousin's death!   (3.5.78–86)

We have come full circle: Juliet speaks of "venging" but means "loving." As Juliet initially separated Romeo the person from the enemy Montague, separating him from the family history of misdeeds to rebaptize him as Love, so after his misdeed, again she sunders him from the category of villain. As she once gave her love completely, so now she forgives him completely. "God pardon him; I do with all my heart."

Amid this new distress, the young Juliet desperately seeks understanding:

JULIET   O sweet my mother, cast me not away!

But her mother heartlessly does just that:

CAPULET'S WIFE   Talk not to me, for I'll not speak a word,
    Do as thou wilt, for I have done with thee.   (3.5.199–204)

Juliet cannot talk to her mother, her father, or even, after her Nurse fails her utterly, to the only close companion she has known. None offer succor, none understanding.

JULIET   Comfort me, counsel me.
    Alack, alack, that heaven should practise stratagems
    Upon so soft a subject as myself.
    What sayst thou? hast thou not a word of joy?
    Some comfort, Nurse.   (3.5.209–13)

Her Nurse fails her: "Go, counselor, | Thou and my bosom henceforth shall be twain" (3.5.240–1). The Friar fails Romeo: "tell me no more." Henceforth, Juliet and Romeo are progressively isolated, separated from the wider world to their own world.

This isolation is a kind of social martyrdom that they already incur before their physical martyrdom. Still, death hovers throughout their romance. When Juliet learns Romeo is banished, she wants to die; when she learns that her father demand she marry another, she wants to die and takes a potion that could well kill her; when Romeo is banished, he wants to die and when he is told his beloved is dead, he takes his own life. She is unable to live without him, and his devotion matches hers. With so much allusion to death in the play, some critics have seen their love as bound up with a (pathological) death wish that finally triumphs in their suicides. They have cited the medieval tradition of ecstatic love that binds passionate love to death, a wounding, as in the imagery of Hugh of St. Victor, seeing in it a kind of warning toward the more moderate love the Friar urges.[21] This lightning passion has been described by Pierre Rousselot as one of the two dominant Christian theologies of love in the Middle Ages, a love that sacrifices the self and its interests to bond wholly with another.

It is violent because it runs counter to those appetites and tyrannizes them. Indeed it seems it could only be satisfied by the destruction of the loving subject, by its absorption in the object loved. Being such, love has no other aim than itself and everything in the human being is sacrificed for its sake, including happiness and reason.[22]

But there is a counter-reading of such passionate romantic love: not that it *courts* death, but that it *overcomes* all limitations, including death. The manner in which Romeo and Juliet are joined, with the tomb as marriage bed, suggests just such triumph over the separation of death.

One of the greatest hurdles their love overcomes is social hatred. For all of its passion, isolation, and hovering mortality, the remarkable strength of Romeo and Juliet's love does more than bind the lovers together in a fatal ending. It also heals the ancient strife. This is vital to the plot. Any such social healing is markedly absent from the later *King Lear*, but here, "The swift and violent passion of Romeo and Juliet is the answering force to their parents' furious and violent hate. Hate kills the lovers, but love, the love of heaven, redressing order and restoring concord through the love of Romeo and Juliet, triumphs over the hate which has endangered the peace of Verona."[23] That the intimate private love of two adolescents could heal public political strife seemed not only improbable to my pragmatic law students, but impossible. "All you need is love"; they sang the Beatles' song to me in jest. But then, they lacked the world view that makes this intelligible, one in which all social concord is grounded in divine love, a love humans can participate in. Such a view allows *Romeo and Juliet* to be like a "microhistory" of how enmity can be reconciled: a process that begins by reframing the enemy and is sustained by forgiving him.

The drama ends with a bold and risky artistic decision: to retell the plot the audience has already witnessed. The filmmaker Zeffirelli lopped it off, and thereby changed the entire meaning of the story. For the tale that the Friar tells the assembled mourners, of steadfast love and holy marriage, of ready forgiveness and mutual suffering, changes the parents' hearts, improbably ending their endless strife. The telling of the narrative gives it political force. It is as if Shakespeare offers a play within the play to show us—almost didactically (is this why Zeffirelli left it out?)—the transformative ethical power a play can have on an audience, here, of assembled mourners. In *Lear*, he leaves any such transformation to the theater audience; instead of witnessing the pain of the grieving parents in *Romeo and Juliet*, in *Lear* that pain is given to us, and when we leave the theater, we must take up the work of social healing after witnessing the whole world erode before our eyes.

As such, love in *Romeo and Juliet* is not fully comprehended by the category of "ecstatic love" after all. It better expresses the understanding proposed by Aquinas. He wrote of the reconciliation of love of self and love of another, of self-interest and altruism, and the way in which what is good for the self is consistent with, rather than in conflict with, what is good for another. He sees all beings contributing to a whole, and all as naturally loving what is good for the whole. For Aquinas, that good is ultimately the love of God, to whom all things owe their being. Self-love, neighbor-love, and God-love are on a continuum in his thought.[24] In a telling analogy, he describes how, sometimes, the hand must be injured to protect the head:

But we see that each part, by a kind of natural inclination, works for the good of the whole, even to its own danger or detriment, for example when someone exposes his hand to a sword to defend his head on which his whole body's health depends. So it is natural that any part in its way loves the whole more than itself. And also according to this natural inclination and according to political virtue, the good citizen faces the danger of death for the common good.[25]

Romeo and Juliet ends, not at the private suicides of the lovers (as it could have), but with the public narrative of their love and suffering, a story that reframes the past events under the banner of love, enabling forgiveness and effectively healing the broken community, reconciling old enemies—a task, by the way, that the state, the Prince with his lawful threats, was powerless to achieve.

CAPULET: O brother Montague, give me thy hand.   (5.3.296)

The Montagues and the Capulets now see people who suffer, who need succor, where they had once seen only enemies. Romeo and Juliet's love is not only private; it is political. That love is not feeble; rather, despite formidable obstacles, that "love never fails" (1 Cor. 13:8).

IV

The Economics of Love

One of the fellows in residence at the Institute for Advanced Study
of Culture at the University of Virginia, Geoffrey Claussen, was
giving a seminar on his research into a rather obscure figure in the
history of thought, one Rabbi Simḥah Zissel Ziv, who lived in Lithuania
and Latvia from 1824 to 1898. Simḥah Zissel was one of the leaders of
the Musar movement, a pietist movement led by a charismatic Rabbi,
Israel Salanter, who focused on the disciplined cultivation of moral
virtue in the Yeshivas. Geoff Claussen, a deep thinker, was writing a
whole book on this figure, so I looked forward to his seminar, to learning something altogether new. What happened was more like a bolt of
lightning: here, in the thought of this nineteenth-century Lithuanian
rabbi, was everything I had been raised to believe. The chief virtue
was love: studying morality was fine, but what really matters is love.
That love demands specific external behavior—caring for the sick,
ensuring the safety of travelers, feeding the poor, etc.—but also "intense
compassion."[1]

Love, in Hebrew *ahavah* or *hesed*, culminates in good deeds, says
Simḥah Zissel. "Polemicizing against 'philosophers' who value con-
templation but devalue action, he argues also against opponents of the
Musar movement who strongly privileged the study of Talmud over
the performance of good deeds," said Claussen. This involved not only
those deeds legislated by the Torah, but more, "To seek out an opportunity for lovingkindness each day...".[2] This was the daily diet my
mother fed us. Like my mother, Simḥah Zissel did not worry about
what preoccupies moral philosophers: who is going to be the benefi-
ciary of this lovingkindness, who will be in and who out. Or for that

matter, the quantity question: how much or how little to give. There was no need to draw a circle around giving, to apportion it. "The prime foundation in a person's life is that he instill in his heart true love of human beings [*ahavat adam*], whatever religion they may be, because the entire political community is a partnership."[3] This love was also, like my mother's, uninfected by particularism.

Furthermore, Simḥah Zissel understood love as having practical economic consequences. These pre-date, by a century, the findings of, for example, Stefano Zamagni in his *Civil Economy*: the insight that the economy runs better on mutual trust than on the presupposition of distrust. Simḥah Zissel writes: "partners, if they want to succeed, must each do his work for his fellow faithfully, for if one makes shoes for his fellow fraudulently, his fellow will reciprocate accordingly with clothing made fraudulently, and so everyone will act this way."[4]

According to classical economics, when you go to the butcher and buy something from him, he doesn't care about you and you don't care about him: it's just an exchange. But more recent economists have argued that what is exchanged with the butcher is not only meat, but good will and trust. In the course of the transaction, the butcher and client are building a bond, and such bonds form networks of trust in the community he serves, a trust that is more important than the specific exchange.

Ethics based on love suggests that when you give, you do not exhaust your supply, that the more you give the more you have. But how do we apply this noble idea to human relations that are not only non-material but also material? What does it mean to translate an ethic of giving into economic terms? In sixteenth- and seventeenth-century England, that project was explicit. In *The English Usurer* (1634), John Blaxton wrote, "Every man is to his neyghbour a debtor, not onely of that which himselfe borroweth, but of what his neyghbour needeth."[5] As Craig Muldrew has shown in his *Economy of Obligation*, "personal social relations were seen in terms of trust, but as market competition and disputes became common, 'society' came to be defined, not just as the positive expression of social unity through Christian love and ritual as had been the case in medieval England, but increasingly as the cumulative unity of the millions of interpersonal obligations which were continually being exchanged and renegotiated." This sociability of commerce made economic transactions a vehicle for trust: "we have no cause to make a Market a place of meer deceit, where every one saith, Trust not me, and I will not trust thee."[6] Reference to self-interest and self-love were predominantly negative before the end of the eighteenth century.[7] Thomas Wilson voiced a sentiment that echoes the Bible and Cicero when he writes in his *Arte of Rhetorique*, "For if I shoulde wholly mynde myne own ease, and folowe gaine without respect to [others], why should not others use the same libertie, and so every man for hymselfe, and the devil for us al, catche that catche may?"[8] His equation of justice with love invokes the biblical love command: "Christes will is suche that we shoulde love God above al thinges and our neighbour as our self. Ther if we do not justice (wherein love doeth consist) we do neither love man, nor yet love God."[9] In Thomas Elyot's *The Boke Named the Governour* (1531), he joins Cicero's notion of justice as keeping faith to the biblical injunction to love the neighbor:

Reason biding him do the same thing to another that thou would have done to the society (without which man's life is unplesant and full of anguish) says, Love thou they neighbor as thou does thyself. And that sentence or precept came from heaven, which society was first ordained of god.[10]

With the rapid rise of court proceedings, this mechanism of trust began to be accompanied by one of law: the contract no longer only sealed mutual trust, in time, it came to be based on protecting self-interest instead of being other-regarding; at its best, *mutual self*-interest, but this is a far cry from ascertaining the needs of others and responding to them.

But what happens when the model of infinite giving from an infinite supply is worked through economics? The first reaction of any pragmatic economist would be that we do not have an infinite supply. Jesus can multiply loaves and fishes and God can rain manna from heaven but neither describes the human condition. So, what are these stories about? Are the loaves and fishes and the manna only metaphors for the spiritual condition? The Hebrews were starving in the wilderness when God rained manna from heaven and the people needed to be fed when Jesus multiplied loaves and fishes. He doesn't multiply ideas; he doesn't multiply the bonds of friendship; he doesn't multiply hope. He specifically gives them material sustenance. Both stories insist on evoking feeding, our most fundamental material need. In the end, can they teach economics anything? One lesson may be that a finite supply is something that we humans create by hoarding our resources, by concentrating goods in a few people, so that the others don't get enough. Such ill-conceived unequal distribution is not inevitable.

Moses said to them, "It is the bread the Lord has given you to eat. This is what the Lord has commanded: 'Everyone is to gather as much as they need. Take an omer for each person you have in your tent.'" The Israelites did as they were told; some gathered much, some little. And when they measured it by the omer, the one who gathered much did not have too much, and the one who gathered little did not have too little. Everyone had gathered just as much as they needed. Then Moses said to them, "No one is to keep any of it until morning." However, some of them paid no attention to Moses; they kept part of it until morning, but it was full of maggots and began to smell. So Moses was angry with them. (Exod. 16:15–20, NIV translation)

We do not even know what human life would look like if there were a fair distribution of goods. We do not know if there is enough food to prevent starvation. What we do know is that by participating in a common activity of giving you end up receiving, because others are giving too. People do not just endlessly take things, they also give, things circulate, best described as a model of a circulating economy of goods.

Most theories of charity as benevolence now separate the sphere of economic contract based on self-interest from the benevolence we exercise toward those in need. But the truth is that everybody is in need. Need is the human condition. No one can live without having basic needs met, and the biblical stories express this. The model that the tradition of love proposes, of giving, has similarities to Adam Smith's but from an opposite motive, that is, instead of everyone acting in self-interest and anticipating that the market will correct itself, the consequence of everyone giving to another is to achieve such a balance. With all giving, and none hoarding, wealth circulates, like love.

Simḥah Zissel understands that giving inspires more giving, that trust inspires more trust, and that love inspires more love. He does not view giving as self-sacrifice, but as motivating reciprocity. This is not simply instrumentality cloaking itself in benevolence; rather, his vision of reciprocity is both caring and pragmatic. He offers a remarkably succinct vision of economic exchange: "[My fellowmen] are my partners, and they prepare for me what I need, and I also prepare for them, with love, what they need . . . If you deal with them faithfully, they will also deal with you faithfully. If you prepare your hearts to love your fellows, they will also prepare their hearts to love you."[11] It is the degradation of this possibility that Shakespeare's *The Merchant of Venice* explores so compellingly in a contract between partners who have no trust, no good will, and no love. The play shows forcefully that partners who enter into a contract really need trust more than law to regulate their behavior.

How could this remote nineteenth-century Lithuanian thinker be in such harmony with my own mother's ethics? I began to suspect something very eerie had happened, that the ideas of Simḥah Zissel and like-minded thinkers may well have been in circulation, not only in Lithuania, but also in my grandmother's home in Latvia, and that she brought those ethics with her when she boarded the boat, alone, at 16 years old, for Richmond, Virginia, on the last day of the month that her ticket was good.[12] I had often felt twinges of envy for those who knew any historical details about their ancestors, as I had only the Sabbath candlestick my grandmother had brought on the boat along with a few goose down pillows that she had stowed in her chest for a dowry. That was it, that was all we had of our past. Not her narrative of suffering and tragedy—resolutely refusing to speak of this, she made sure that pain was not passed along. But now, I had been given the most important thing of all, the foundation itself, the code of ethics embraced by my family. What I did know was that despite her hardships—her reluctant leave-taking of the father she would never see again, and the sisters who had stayed behind with their children, all murdered in pogroms—love was always the meaning of life for her, and that meant daily acts of loving-kindness, tireless giving. She was of one of the poorest of Dayton's families, but every Friday, she baked bread and as a little girl, my mother passed it out from a basket in the neighborhood. The strength of that ethic was unwavering. So, perhaps my quest for a richer understanding of justice than those offered by philosophy or political thought had brought me to this Institute to work on a book on love and justice, and strangely, to a young scholar named Geoffrey Claussen who was assigned to the office right next to mine where he worked away tirelessly on obscure Hebrew texts, only to give me, in what I could only discern was an act of loving generosity, the remarkable gift of the wellspring of my otherwise erased family heritage.[13]

It turns out that even on the subject of human nature, I could glean support from this thinker so remote, both historically and intellectually, from my American education in English literature, Christian theology, and Classical philosophy. Simḥah Zissel's ethic of giving rests upon a natural goodness in human nature, a goodness expressed in sympathy and compassion; indeed, an instinct to give and to protect others that is as strong as the instinct to preserve oneself.[14]

Hobbes regarded fear for our own preservation as our chief sentiment, believing that we will even submit to a tyrant if he promises to preserve us. But, as Ian Baucom has written, "perhaps the opening articulation of a politics of love is to refuse that offer of exchange, through which our various states, commonwealths, and sovereign authorities make us safe from fear if we will license them to quarantine (or annihilate) all that we have been instructed to hold inimical to ourselves. This politics asks that we refuse to abandon love as, itself, a fearsome thing... more than capable of reminding us that in our lives as subjects and as citizens we are, and continue to be, 'fluid and permeable.'"[15]

The belief in natural goodness, while part of my mother's legacy, has precious little support from the mainstream tradition of western philosophy, which says we need reason to guide us, reason purified of any inclinations, passions, sentiments, interests, a reason that can develop universal maxims to guide our moral life, and is even a far cry from the strains in Christian thought that stress original sin over original goodness, a human depravity resulting from Adam's disobedience. Still, despite the strong cultural currency of those traditions, I was raised to believe in the fundamental goodness of people. People could disappoint, of course, but when people were less than good, that was because they were injured, they had suffered, and this was why compassion—even for people who committed horrible deeds, especially for them—was in order. This meant I had no trouble with Jesus's command to "love the enemy" but I was quite confused by Aristotle's belief that to live a good life, we help friends and harm enemies.

Here is Rabbi Simḥah Zissel (sounding just like my mother):

the truth is thus: that it is possible for a person to reach the height of virtue. For it is not as most people think: that a person is a person and it is good for him to learn to become an angel. This is not so. Rather, on the contrary, a person is truly an angel... This is as scripture says; "I had said that you are angels" (Psalm 82:6). Thus it is better to learn when one is young, for then the animal within one will not grow further.[16]

Often, theologians want to stress the difference between divine love, infinite, universal, and human love, finite, infected by self-preservation.

In Simḥah Zissel's vision of man as an angel, God's love does not cor-rect or compensate for human limitation or depravity; instead, divine love is the source of the human capacity to love. "God loves all crea-tures; were it not so, they could not exist in the world." Simḥah Zissel cites this biblical verse to affirm that all the desires of all creatures are satisfied by the infinite love of God: "You open up your hands and satisfy the desire of all that lives" (Psalm 145:16).[17]

Contracts and Justice

In our time, it is difficult to think about justice or to imagine a civil sphere without contracts, even to think of a free society without the concept. "Our freedom of contract, both the freedom to enter into legally binding agreements that advance our own purposes, and the freedom to avoid obligations unless we express our consent, is a key organizing principle of a free society."[18] Contracts govern all manner of interpersonal transactions: we make contracts with the landlord, the health insurance company, with the cellphone provider.

In a larger sense, the modern liberal social imaginary puts contracts at the center of a just society. Since Rousseau, Locke, and Kant, political thinking has imagined an original contract in which members of the community freely enter into a social contract that encodes their con-cepts of justice. Their principles of justice are forged by an imagined original agreement, "in which those who engage in social cooperation choose together, in one joint act, the principles which are to assign basic rights and duties, and to determine the division of social benefits."[19] Furthermore, according to Rawls, the imaginary contract requires that "a group of persons must decide once and for all what is to count among them as just and unjust" and the principles that will "regulate all subsequent criticism and reform of institutions."[20] Contracts have been seen as no less than the solution to domination.

With so much invested in the concept of contractual justice, it is worthwhile to inquire further about the nature of a contract, to explore the relation between justice and the fundamental presupposi-tions of contracts. The textbook definition is this: "A contract is a promise that the law will enforce." It has two components, as Michael Sandel has summarized: first, someone enters into a contract freely

choosing to do so. The moral force of the contract is derived from its
voluntary basis, that I choose to enter it, freely, binding myself in the
obligation. "When I enter freely into an agreement, I am bound by its
terms, whatever they may be. Whether its provisions are fair or inequi-
table, favorable or harsh, I have 'brought them on myself.' "[21] Under the
condition of voluntary obligation, the procedure itself determines
fairness: it is fair if I entered into it freely. This emphasis on freedom
explains why contracts are considered the backbone of liberal thought.
The second understanding stresses reciprocity: ideally, the terms of a
contract promote *mutual* benefit. Both parties should gain in some
commensurate way. "With reciprocity, the emphasis is less on the fact
of my agreement than on the benefits I enjoy; contracts bind not
because they are willingly incurred but because (or in so far as) they
tend to produce results that are fair."[22] But "fairness" must be a standard
independent of the contract for us to be able to judge if the contract
is fair, if it is mutually beneficial.

The moral incompleteness of each model is highlighted by the existence of
the other. I may be bound by my voluntarily made obligations but they may
be unfair OR I may be bound by a fair deal that I could have entered into
with constraints, essentially unfreely. In practice, agreements turn out unfairly
for a variety of reasons... One or the other party may be coerced or otherwise
disadvantaged in his bargaining position, or misled or otherwise misinformed
about the value of the objects being exchanged, or confused or mistaken
about his own needs and interest, or where uncertain future returns are
involved, a bad judge of risk, and so on.... However strictly one defines the
requirements of a voluntary agreement, the fact that different persons are sit-
uated differently will assure that some differences of power and knowledge
persist...[23]

When we think about the justice of contracts, then, we do it from
two points of view: the *conditions* under which the agreement was
made—whether voluntarily or under some coercion, and the *terms* of
the agreement—whether the terms are fair. While the first is a question of procedure, it still allows us to ask if the terms are fair, and that
requires an appeal to some standard of fairness beyond the contract.
Among others, John Rawls "emphasizes that, notwithstanding their
voluntary dimension, our actual obligations are never born of consent
alone but inevitably presuppose an antecedent background morality,
independently derived, in the light of which it is always possible to ask
whether one ought to have consented or not."[24] As Cassandra says in

Shakespeare's *Troilus and Cressida*, "It is the purpose that makes strong the vow, | But vows to every purpose must not hold."

Contracts harbor further perils that lurk in that very definition: "A contract is a *promise* that the law will enforce." Those of us who are attentive to language know that a promise is a very slippery act of speech: If you jokingly ask me to marry you, you are not offering a proposal of marriage.[25] So how do we know what we are consenting to when we enter a contract? Not only the complexity of ascertaining the meaning of the promise, but something further about a promise is troubling. There is no speech event that requires more trust than a promise. If I describe the present, you can decide if my description is adequate or not, but when I promise, I speak of the future, and for my words to carry force, you need to trust what I say about the future. For Hannah Arendt, promising "serves to set up in the ocean of uncertainty, which the future is by definition, islands of security without which not even continuity, let alone durability of any kind, would be possible in the relationships between men."[26] However, contracts implicitly presuppose distrust for they must be upheld by the mechanisms of law; again, "a contract is a promise that the *law* will enforce." How it will enforce that promise is troubling enough; that it presumes to enforce something as complex as a promise is more troubling still. No small part of the trouble with contracts is that they have been credited as able to do more than their limited purview; beyond the specificity of their agreed upon exchange, they cannot create trust between parties, they cannot create enduring bonds, they cannot heal enmity. Relying overmuch on contracts for social bonds is bound to be disappointing. Nonetheless, both our commerce and our concept of a just society rest on this deeply vexed concept.[27]

The Price of Love: *The Merchant of Venice*

Shakespeare was remarkably attuned to the troubles that plague contractual thinking. In *The Merchant of Venice*, contractual thinking is called upon to govern both justice and love. Promises are made contractually, vengeance is sought contractually, social healing is instigated contractually, and in all cases, the solutions offered by those contracts fall far short of the aspirations of either justice or love. The play explores the fiction that contracts are entered into freely (there is no real autonomy under regimes of oppression) and the fiction that they encode fairness as mutual benefit. Above all, the trust that must attend promises is completely absent, and the law is exposed as powerless to enforce such trust.

While Shakespeare's plays often draw heavily upon both legal and religious thought to animate the problem of justice, he puts versions of both Jewish and Christian ideas of justice into explicit dialogue in *The Merchant of Venice*, and as if that were not complex enough, he heaps common law and equity courts into the mix. Hence, we find both of the following declarations of excess in the critical literature: on the one hand, "in this play, the advocate of Shakespeare's exceptional Biblical knowledge will find more material than in any others,"[28] and on the other hand, "over the centuries, the *Merchant of Venice* has spawned more commentary by lawyers than any other Shakespeare play."[29]

Some critics have lumped together Judaism, justice, and law on the one hand, and pitted them against faith, love, and charity, on the other, in a seeming echo of Paul. Many read the play as an endorsement of Christian triumphalism—showing how Christian love and mercy must supersede Jewish justice. The Christian mercy argument blurs into equity law which then seems to "win" in a contest with civil law, or does it?[30] Others have argued that the play's message is that Jewish law should not be altogether dispensed with, only mitigated by the Christian charity that supersedes it.[31] But these may risk being too tidy.

Such readings can over-simplify the complexities of this play's stunning multi-layered critique, one which extends to Christianity—after all, the challenge of Christian justice, "love thy enemy," is not achieved in this drama, Judaism—Shylock's retributive justice knows no forgiveness, equity—which favors the aristocracy, civil law—which can be brutally literal, commerce—which reduces love to transactions and inevitably broken promises, and contracts, whose stipulations of free consent and fairness are travestied.

The contract in *The Merchant of Venice* is neither freely entered— Antonio does not believe the terms are fully serious, nor does he accurately assess the risk to his fortunes, so he enters the contract blindly, not freely—nor are the terms fair; the threat to his life if he cannot repay the loan is absurd. As Salerio says to Shylock, "Why, I am sure if he forfeit thou wilt not take his flesh. What's that good for?" (3.1.46–7). If a contract is ideally based on mutual benefit, in this drama, the contract is instead an opportunity for unilateral harm. But if the notion of freely entered contracts is critiqued, so too is the alternative relation, domination, for triumphalist justice is exposed as a fiction when Portia and the court turn against Shylock ruthlessly, stripping him not only of his funds but his identity.

The criticism on *The Merchant of Venice* is a tribute not only to the complexity of the play but also to how fruitful criticism can be; for centuries, scholars have engaged in a lively debate on the legal, religious, social, economic, and political dimensions of the play. For Harold Bloom, "The play, honestly interpreted and responsibly performed...would no longer be acceptable on a stage in New York City, for it is an anti-Semitic masterpiece, unmatched in its kind." For Daniel Kornstein, "Rather than anti-Semitic, the play can be read as pro-minority rights. It shows how inequality before the law breeds dangerous and divisive discontent."[32] The *Merchant's* performance history notably includes stagings in Nazi Germany as well as in the newly forged state of Israel. Portia has been embraced as a paragon of skill, wit, and learning who commands authority as both lawyer and judge in a man's world,[33] and Portia has been reviled: "In addition to her hypocrisy and vindictiveness, we see her as a bigot, and not just a minor-league bigot, but a world-class, equal opportunity hate monger."[34] In the early nineteenth century, William Hazlitt dismissed Portia more politely, but as definitively: "Portia is not a great favorite with us."

The pivotal trial scene produces the most haunting image in the history of literature for reducing the human person to property: the pound of flesh that Shylock demands as payment for a forfeited loan. His determination to seek justice in the form of this obscene payment makes a travesty of damages in contract law. Portia, disguised as the wise lawyer, hoists him on his own petard, famously pushing his literalism about the penalty for the broken contract even farther than he does:

PORTIA   A pound of that same merchant's flesh is thine,
   The court awards it, and the law doth give it.
SHYLOCK   Most rightful judge!
PORTIA   And you must cut this flesh from off his breast,
   The law allows it, and the court awards it.
SHYLOCK   Most learned judge! A sentence, come prepare.
PORTIA   Tarry a little, there is something else,—

> This bond doth give thee here no jot of blood,
> The words expressly are "a pound of flesh":
> Take then thy bond, take thou thy pound of flesh,
> But in the cutting it, if thou dost shed
> One drop of Christian blood, thy lands and goods
> Are (by the laws of Venice) confiscate
> Unto the state of Venice.
>   .   .   .   .
> For, as thou urgest justice, be assur'd
> Thou shalt have justice more than thou desir'st.   (4.1.296–314)

Flaunting any interest in verisimilitude, the play quickly turns Shylock from a plaintiff in a civil suit into a defendant in a criminal trial, and by doing so, brilliantly represents the confusion wrought by seeking justice through a measurable compensation. Shylock, intent upon murdering Antonio out of revenge for all of the degradations he has endured from him and his Christian friends—including the theft of his daughter by a Christian—wants to use the law to execute that vengeance. But how far is this murderous literalism being associated with Jewish law, hence, with Judaism? Are we seeing Paul's dictum dramatized that the "letter (that is, the old law of Moses) killeth but the spirit (the new law of Christ) maketh live"? Paul's characterization of Pharisaic literalism fueled anti-Semitism in the Renaissance and doubtless contributed to this portrait of the Jew—as not only the avaricious cheating money-lender, but the legalistic one.[35] But in reality, Judaism is hardly silent about killing: from the biblical story of the first two brothers, Cain's slaying of Abel, on through the revelation of the law in Exodus, Levitical legislation, and biblical prophecy, killing is expressly forbidden. Vengeance is the Lord's, not man's prerogative. Surely, Shylock's murderousness is not "Jewish justice."

To ensnare Shylock in his understanding of literal justice, Portia pushes the letter of the law to its utmost extreme:

> Therefore prepare thee to cut off the flesh.—
> Shed thou no blood, nor cut thou less nor more
> But just a pound of flesh. If thou tak'st more
> Or less than a just pound, be it but so much
> As makes it light or heavy in the substance
> Or the division of the twentieth part
> Of one poor scruple, nay, if the scale do turn
> But in the estimation of a hair,
> Thou diest, and all thy goods are confiscate.   (4.1.320–8)

Measuring is mocked as a tool of justice: "the twentieth part of one poor scruple...the estimation of a hair."

Shylock is not seeking redress from rabbinic law, but from a secular Venetian court of law, and his working assumption is that if his claim is not honored, if contracts are not honored, then the entire legal structure that protects all of Venice's international commerce will crumble. His insistence on literal justice is aligned to common law. In his opening speech at court, commingling allusions to oaths and curses in Judaism with the secular court and state, he sees that freedom rests upon contracts that bind:

> by our holy Sabbath I have sworn
> To have the due and forfeit of my bond.—
> If you deny it, let the danger light
> Upon your charter and your city's freedom!   (4.1.36–9)

If the dominant critical commonplace that sees the play representing Christian triumphalism were right, then the dead letter of the law, literalism, is not only embraced by Judaism, but *also* by common law: and *both* are being subjected to critique. Several legal studies have read Portia's victory in the trial as an endorsement of Shakespeare's belief that common law's over-strict justice needs to be mitigated by equity.[36] In that reading, Christian mercy trumps Jewish justice, it is exercised by equity courts that trump common law, and Portia is their spokesman.

But critics who are especially sensitive to the economic and political context in which the play was written have offered another perspective, commercial:

as the complex, large-scale financial operations of early capitalism began to emerge in the middle years of the 16th century, its practitioners became acutely aware of the value of a comprehensive and predictable legal system that offered protection from arbitrary interference...The common law, particularly after it began to recognize and incorporate the jurisprudence of the increasingly important international mercantile legal system, was clearly the law that best offered this protection.[37]

The social conflict between the interests of the rising middle class, on the one hand, and those of the Crown and landowners, on the other, forms the socio-economic backdrop of the play.

This is a profound play about commerce—it is called the *merchant* of Venice, not the Jew of Venice (and it could have been, Marlowe gave us the Jew of Malta). In its world of nascent global capitalism, the activities of the rising merchant class were protected by common law; it also protected their profits from exploitation by the Crown and the landed aristocracy. In this light, "while the immediate stakes in the conflict between the two groups were financial, the ultimate prize was much greater: the ability of the independent rising class to use the common law to thwart the sociopolitical will of the ruling class."[38] It did this by enforcing contracts. Thank goodness for contracts and for the law that enforces them—or so it seems to these economically-minded critics.

But, of course, the aristocracy were not inclined to be so easily restrained. "Equity courts," whose authority was granted by the Crown, became the chief means by which the landed class and monarch could exercise their prerogatives. With the language of mercy, equity law allowed landholders to slip out of the reach of common law. It is likely that Shakespeare's audience would not have heard Portia's famous speech on mercy as the timeless embrace of transcendent Christian ideals that later audiences have. Even in recent productions, many directors slow the speech down to make her seem to intone eternal verities; in film versions, close-ups seem irresistible.

> The quality of mercy is not strain'd,
> It droppeth as the gentle rain from heaven
> Upon the place beneath: it is twice blest,
> It blesseth him that gives and him that takes.
> 'Tis mightiest in the mightiest, it becomes
> The throned monarch better than his crown.
> His sceptre shows the force of temporal power,
>
> .   .   .   .
>
> But mercy is above this sceptred sway,
> It is enthroned in the hearts of kings,
> It is an attribute to God himself;
> And earthly power doth then show likest God's
> When mercy seasons justice... (4.1.180–93)

The speech which seems to endorse Christian mercy is immediately undercut by talk of "mitigating justice": "I have spoke thus much | To mitigate the justice of thy plea." Shakespeare's audiences would have understood that this language of "mitigating the law or justice" was the language of equity, an aristocratic prerogative that flowed from the doctrine of divine kingship, and that unlike "the gentle rain that droppeth from heaven," it did not fall on everyone. Instead, it protected the landed nobility.

In this light, Shylock is not only espousing the value of law, but also the rights of minorities to be protected by law. The Jewish Shylock, as the archetypal outsider in Christian Renaissance Venice, is asking for protection from the ruling class. He asks the wrong person. Portia speaks of mercy, but indulges instead in the strictest interpretation of the law, and far from granting mercy, she indicts Shylock as a criminal, strips him of his property, and endorses his forced conversion.[39] In the course of Portia's speech, what begins with pious talk of God becomes degraded to the instrument of aristocratic oppression of minorities. Genuine mercy does not mitigate justice: it fulfills it.

Furthermore, her speech, so often taken as an exemplum of Christian virtue—even if it is the preamble to "mountainish inhumanity" as Thomas More describes intolerance to aliens—is, ironically enough, drawn from the "old" rather than the "new" testament. Its chief inspirations are: "My doctrine shall drop as the rain, my speech shall distil as the dew, as the small rain upon the tender herb, and as the showers upon the grass" (Deut. 32:2); "O how fair a thing is mercy in the time of anguish and trouble! It is like a cloud of rain, that comes in the time of a drought" (Eccles. 36:19; and see Eccles. 28:1–4). Christian mercy is after all an inheritance of Jewish mercy. The play is thereby questioning or at least "putting under quotation marks the customary equation of the Old Law with strict judgment and the New Law with spiritual mercy."[40] Similarly, when the mercy that structures the doctrine of grace in Christianity is manipulated by courts of equity law, it can be reduced to protecting landowners' interests, rather than granting universal mercy. Once the trial ends with no mercy for Shylock, we see how fully the potentially inspiring biblical language of mercy had been degraded by Portia. But the devil can cite scripture.

But while this play may ironically question the rhetoric of Christian mercy as harboring potentially vindictive acts, its purpose is surely not a defense of Judaism—for all its sympathy to Shylock as an alien who does not enjoy the protection of Venetian society.[41] If Portia reduces mercy to mitigation to ruthlessness, Jewish law suffers a similar degradation by Shylock: surely demanding justice while intending vengeful murder is contrary to every version of the law—and there are many— that the Hebrew Bible offers. In Exodus 34, the law against murder takes a particularly poignant turn when Moses is summarizing the law and concludes with the sublime metaphor for injustice: "you shall not boil a kid in its mother's milk." Far from the kind of legalistic prescription that has been made of this about dietary laws and how a particularist community embraces them while sacrificing true justice, Moses is insisting, according to the rabbis, that you should not deal death with the vehicle for life. "Don't boil a kid in its mother's milk" is not a bad way of thinking about the law. Use this potential instrument for social health, for sustenance, for life, instead of for social injury, vengeance, and death.

When the religious covenant that binds justice to law is stripped of its transcendent underpinnings of the love command, and becomes secular contract, it is at risk of being reduced to literalism, mere procedure, and losing sight of fairness. Surely Shylock has lost his bearings. Another way to say this is that at the disenchantment of the world from the belief that its order is founded and governed by transcendent goodness, religious rhetoric—including the language of mercy, law, justice, faith, contracts, and oaths—can be readily hijacked for political and economic interests. Is Shakespeare's play suggesting that the secular law (both common law and equity) falls short of religious law? I doubt that. For both law and religion are subjected to critique. In both, appearances deceive; all that glitters is not gold. Shakespeare says this better:

> The world is still deceiv'd with ornament—
> In law, what plea so tainted and corrupt
> But being season'd with a gracious voice
> Obscures the show of evil? In religion,
> What damned error but some sober brow
> Will bless it, and approve it with a text,
> Hiding the grossness with fair ornament?
> There is no vice so simple, but assumes
> Some mark of virtue on his outward parts... (3.2.74–82)

Both law and religion can be misused by vice. The play seems acutely aware that once a worldview that anchors right and wrong, good and evil, is unmoored, and a commercial worldview takes hold instead, we should be wary of the results. Moreover, it explores the price of reducing the world, life, and love, to the calculus of economic gain. No ascetic, Shakespeare was a businessman who was among the first to organize his players into a company in which he owned the principal share. That company, the Chamberlain's Men, took out loans in order to build their theater, the Globe, and it was encumbered by interest payments. According to court records, Shakespeare's father was brought to court for demanding too much interest (English law provided that 10 per cent interest was acceptable). While the Bible and the Church Fathers condemned usury, Calvin thought it inevitable in the modern world. Perhaps because Shakespeare had experienced the complexities of capitalism and the legal system, he issues the caution that both economics and law can be powerful instruments of injustice, especially against the interests of aliens and minorities. In this play, these instruments are cloaked with deadly hypocrisy: legal codes are used to mete out vengeance, the language of mercy is used to degrade, the rhetoric of love is used to commit acts of hatred.

In Renaissance literature, love was frequently spoken of in commercial terms: lovers as free agents giving and receiving with the expectation of increase, the "natural interest" of breeding happiness together. This was joined to a theological discourse of giving a gift with no expectation of return, neither of interest nor of principal—giving recklessly, as Christ did, as Antonio does by offering his life as the bond in his loan from Shylock. The fact that matrimony is a legal contract adds to this picture. Both of the plots in the play, the courtship and marriage to Portia and the loan from Shylock that funds it, explore the economics of human relationships, of giving and receiving. But while love can include a contract and the economic transaction of dowries, surely it is more than that. That reduction of humanity to economic terms is satirized when Shylock learns that his daughter has fled him with a Christian and stolen his money: "My daughter, O my ducats, O my daughter!" (2.8.15–22). Justice is, in theory, protected by law and calculated economically, but perhaps justice, like love, must exceed law and economics—else we would use the law to murder.

But this raises a difficult question, one that should give us pause. Does justice exceed the capacities of the law? Is injury to a person's dignity beyond the purview of law to repair? In the trial scene, law is manipulated by Shylock to get revenge on the enemies who have degraded him, and law is manipulated by the enemies not only to disarm but also to destroy him. This most famous trial scene in literature may even be hinting toward legal nihilism. But Shakespeare doesn't sound like a nihilist—at least, not here—for his engagement in social critique suggests his fervent embrace of underlying values that enable these judgments. Surely this play does suggest that human worth is not measurable or translatable into economic terms—My daughter, O my ducats, O my daughter—and further, that commerce, for all its advantages, has a dangerous price—a kind of imperialism or infection that reduces all to its terms. Everything is bought and sold in the mercantile world of Venice, especially love.

When Portia's suitor, Bassanio, first describes his love for Portia to Antonio in order to ask him for funds for courting her, it is in relentlessly economic terms. His vocabulary is laced with terms like "fortunes," "worth," "means" in a web of double entendres.

> In Belmont is a lady richly left,
> And she is fair, and (fairer than that word),
> Of wondrous virtues,
>
> . . . .
>
> Nor is the wide world ignorant of her worth,
> For the four winds blow in from every coast
> Renowned suitors [she attracts international buyers]...
>
> . . . .
>
> O my Antonio, had I but the means
> To hold a rival place with one of them,
> I have a mind presages me such thrift
> That I should questionless be fortunate.   (1.1.161–76)

In such a world, where people are bought and sold, justice is inevitably crafted to compensate economically, for in a world of commerce, this is all we have to redress our injuries. More than a critique of the law, then, perhaps this play is critical of the mentality that reduces all persons, all value, to economic terms. When law, or for that matter, love, succumbs to economy, perhaps it begins to lose some of the value of performing justice—easy to say, for how can law be responsive to injury outside of economic terms? We seek damages for repair of injury; Shylock seeks injury instead of damages. A pound of flesh cannot rectify; it only destroys. And what about damages? What would satisfy Shylock's demand of justice if not the life of Antonio? I asked my students this question, and they said an apology. This is the logic that confession, contrition, and apology achieve healing.[42]

If law can help to protect against social hatred, should law be in the business of promulgating social health, and if so, to what extent and how? Do we need a minimal approach, a protection of our rights: do not steal, do not defame, do not kill? Or do we want to throw into the mix a positive valuation of the other: respect, concern, even love? What kind of law has the biblical tradition given us when it commands that we love the neighbor? Is this the realm of the political?

One of the reasons these questions are urgent is that in secular modernity, we have fallen under precisely the spell that Shakespeare anticipates in *The Merchant of Venice*: the economic model of social relations.[43] This is seen, not as a loss of our humanity, not a terrible compromise of our moral life, not even as tragic. Rather, the economic model is embraced as efficient, useful, even (amazingly enough), just. The influence of a thinker like Richard Posner, who followed his disturbing enough *Economics of Law* with his outrageous *Economics of Justice*, is a symptom of how widespread this cultural blight has become. I need not critique the particulars of his work—economic and legal theorists have done an excellent job, showing how making the accumulation of wealth a normative principle for justice simply does not hold.[44] His claim that "reason" or "scientism" grounds his embrace of the highest good as the maximization of wealth could not offer a better example of the failure of the modern scientific paradigm to protect the moral good. What is most reasonable, for Posner, is to assess, rationally, the costs and benefits of each interaction. These include rape, racial discrimination, even revolution. All have assessable costs and how each is adjudicated can be discerned through reasoned assessment. In an astonishing conflation of the value of charity with wealth, he writes: "even altruism (benevolence) is an economizing principle, because it can be a substitute for costly market and legal processes."[45] In his economic stupor, he has clearly lost his bearings: when charity is cost-effective it is no longer charity. Besides, *caritas*, translated as charity and love, is an intrinsic measure of worth, while price implies an extrinsic one. For Posner, corrective justice serves wealth-maximization, "an act of injustice [is] an act that reduces the wealth of society . . . a failure to rectify such acts would reduce the wealth of society by making such acts more common." Converting social hatred into an economic calculus, an injury into a penalty clause, is precisely what *The Merchant of Venice* mocks in its central image of the pound of flesh. Again, a pound of flesh cannot rectify, and neither can a trove of ducats.

Why does the central plot of *The Merchant of Venice* focus on a contract, a perverse one? Decidedly not to teach us either the right way to make one, assess one, uphold one, or determine the costs and benefits of one. The comic-tragic exaggeration of the penalty clause of a pound of human flesh exposes this contract itself as ludicrous at best, and dehumanizing at worst. Made in the context of social hatred, the contract cannot have any assessable value for the "price" of the Christian hatred and the rage it inspires in Shylock are boundless. Similarly, far from reducing his daughter to his ducats, Shylock's anguished juxtaposition of the two has the effect of reminding us that the loss of his daughter cannot be measured in ducats. During the trial scene, Shylock demonstrates forcefully how untranslatable his pain and his rage are into any price: offered a huge fortune, he insists instead upon the contract—the pound of flesh, the life of Antonio. But this is obscene, and the obscenity deepens when Portia thrusts this logic back at him: not one drop of Christian blood can be shed with the pound of flesh or Shylock loses his life. Far from offering an economic norm for justice, *The Merchant of Venice* constantly holds out prices only to reject them: from the suitors' quest for Portia to Shylock's revenge, from Antonio's love for Bassanio to Bassanio's love of Portia. The gold and silver caskets, the rings, the ducats, the loan, the contract, the ventures of the merchant, the confiscation of Shylock's property: each only suggests in its own way that the world of Shakespeare's imagined Venice, and perhaps by extension, of Shakespeare's very real London, is afflicted with moral and spiritual depravity.

Portia's father explicitly sought to eliminate those who would attach a high payment (or price) to her. He reaches beyond the grave to help his daughter find the worthy partner for her life. He has devised a test—her suitors must choose one of three caskets, of gold, silver, or lead—and the one who wins the test is the one who does not embrace wealth, chooses lead, and is willing to give all and take on unguarded risk. While Antonio loses his fortune at sea, he admits repeatedly that this is meaningless to him. When Portia does give her love a price, of the ring, it is only to discover how readily her husband gives it away. The pricelessness of Shylock's love for his wife Leah is contrasted to the wretchedness of his daughter's exchange of her ring for a monkey. If *The Merchant of Venice* has anything to teach us, it is that the economic understanding of justice is spiritually bankrupt. In a world defined by ventures, usury, contracts, a world of "merchants" in the deepest sense, there is only exploitation. Love, of the neighbor, of the other, of the enemy, romantic love—let alone human compassion—has no place in this economic calculus.

In the midst of this critique, does Shakespeare offer any hope, a recommendation, however faint, of an alternative understanding of justice? Love—not calculable self-interest—is held forth as that positive vision. And as in *King Lear* and *Romeo and Juliet*, love is understood as the fulfillment of justice. In the revelation of the Law, "Mercy and truth are met together; righteousness and peace have kissed each other" (Ps. 85:10).

The justice of love is a radical ethical alternative to the economics of justice, the maximization of wealth. But what does Love have to say about contracts? First, with love, it is not always about freedom. Love itself binds us, obligates us to the well-being of the beloved. When we love another, there are things we must do and things we must not. Freedom is not the point. One could argue that we enter into these obligations freely when we love, so love is much like a contract, but the experience of love is not so bloodless as "freely choosing"—when we love we cannot help but love. Secondly, love is not interested in fairness, if understood as mutual benefit. Indeed, most love relationships could not withstand the test of fairness. Is it fair for a mother to give all to her child? Where is the mutual advantage? For a lover to think of the well-being of his beloved before his own? Assessments are not made, when we love, about whether we are both profiting equally by this love. Neither autonomy nor mutuality are at the forefront when we think about love. When we love, we do not measure our giving and anticipate that the score will be evened. We love whether or not that love is returned.

Love offers a wholly different standard of human value than a contract, one in which the emphasis is neither freedom nor fairness. Rather, to put it simply, it is giving. Shylock's murderous vengeance toward his business partner begs to be set in relief against Rabbi Simḥah Zissel's attitude. "You must prepare your bosom for his knife," Portia tells Shylock's victim, and shortly after, she insists that this pound of flesh, taken near his heart, cannot include a drop of Christian blood or Shylock will be executed. Simḥah Zissel speaks of partnership as infused with trust and love: "[My fellowmen] are my partners, and they prepare for me what I need, and I also prepare for them, with love, what they need...If you deal with them faithfully, they will also deal with you faithfully. If you prepare your hearts to love your fellows they will also prepare their hearts to love you."[46] Prepare your hearts, not for the knife, but for love. This light makes an appearance in this dark play, albeit a brief one: the lead casket has the epigram (one changed by Shakespeare from his source), "he who chooses me hazards all he has." Even that is ironized when a losing suitor complains: What says this leaden casket?

> "Who chooseth me must give and hazard all he hath."
> Must give—for what? for lead, hazard for lead!
> This casket threatens—Men that hazard all
> Do it in hope of fair advantages...   (2.7.16–19)

The worthy lover is willing to give and hazard all, give without measure, risk all, without calculating advantages.

In Paul's hymn of love, 1 Corinthians 13, he defines the ethics of love as internally driven, as the quality that gives value to all of life's activities, as the final ideal of justice. Even acts of goodness "profit nothing" without love, for they are merely external, not driven by moral love and genuine compassion. It is love that defines human relations as generous, tolerant, and forgiving. But it is also a remarkably radical understanding of justice: "Love suffereth long, and is kind; love envieth not... it is not self-seeking, it is not easily angered, it keeps no record of wrongs" (1 Cor. 13:4–5). The record of wrongs is well-kept in Shakespeare's Venice, none are forgotten, none are forgiven. And one wrong only issues in another. The justice of love is one that Shakespeare's play can long for, as an alternative, one that the music of the spheres enjoys in the distant skies, but not one that obtains on our sad planet:

> Such harmony is in immortal souls,
> But whilst this muddy vesture of decay
> Doth grossly close it in, we cannot hear it.   (5.1.63–5)

V

The Forgiveness of Love

> He who fights with monsters should look to it
> that he himself does not become a monster.
>
> NIETZSCHE, *Beyond Good and Evil*

> Do not seek revenge or bear a grudge against anyone among
> your people, but love your neighbor as yourself.
>
> LEVITICUS 19:18

Punishing

Sometimes, justice is an idea that people use to hurt other people. They inflict harm to "satisfy" justice, an odd metaphor suggesting that justice may be hungry and need to be fed some juicy morsels, "satisfied." Nietzsche wrote that high-sounding talk about justice may be only a cover for vindictiveness.

These cellar rodents full of vengefulness and hatred—what have they made of revenge and hatred? Have you heard these words uttered? If you trusted simply to their words, would you suspect you were among men of ressenti-ment? . . . [his interlocutor responds] I understand; I'll open my ears again (oh! oh! oh! And *close* my nose). Now I can really hear what they have been saying all along: "We good men—we are the just—what they desire they call, not retaliation, but 'the triumph of justice'; what they hate is not their enemy, no! they hate 'injustice'. . . " (*On the Genealogy of Morals*, First Essay, §14)

Kant adds, "We like to flatter ourselves with the false claim to a more noble motive, but in fact we can never, even by the strictest examination, completely plumb the depths of the secret incentives of our actions."[1] The kind of justice that would be satisfied by harming another is justice as retribution, and the satisfaction of such justice is achieved by punishment.

What are the chief arguments for retribution? One of the most persistent is that if someone injures another, the injurer *deserves* to be punished. There seems to be a widespread intuition that just as those who do good should be rewarded, so those who do harm should be punished. But why? On what grounds? It turns out that such intuitions rest on surprisingly little grounding. Those who support the idea that we should punish wrongdoers, hurt the hurters, often argue that this desire for retribution is foundational; that is, it needs no further explanation. They describe it as "natural." But without a plausible reason for hurting the injurer, it is not possible to justify.

Just as high-sounding talk of justice may only mask revenge, so high-sounding talk of just punishment often masks responses in excess of the crime. Why do we punish so hard and so much? Why are prisons dehumanizing and over-full? Rage is partly responsible, as well as the culture's ready confusion between wrongful acts and the wrongdoers. This stems from our understanding of the human person. Our criminal justice system is built on the anthropology that humans are freely choosing moral agents. Understanding criminality as taking place in a realm of freedom is part of the liberal story. Its forebear is Kant, who believes the moral law must be followed independent of social context or inclination, that infractions of it must be punished according to the iniquity. His fury is directed, not against the wrongdoer so much as against the injury to the moral order itself. Hence, for the sake of justice, he endorses merciless retribution. Kant's bloodthirsty passages on retribution are in his *Metaphysical Elements of Justice*: "Judicial punishment can never be used merely as a means to promote some other good for the criminal himself or for civil society, but instead it must in all cases be imposed on him only on the ground that he has committed a crime." After all, criminals freely choose to do wrong.

But to what extent is this freedom of choice a fiction? As a noted legal scholar writes, "It is no secret that certain social conditions are 'crimogenic'—that those born to poverty and discrimination are far more likely to offend than those who are raised in or achieve high economic or social status."[2] Nonetheless, "the criminal law system does little to discern how social disadvantage may constrain choice or to think about moral desert in light of social disadvantage."[3] Under the regime of justice that claims to adjudicate right and wrong, some behaviors—regardless of social disadvantages—are considered just wrong. Again, there is rampant confusion of the wrong deed with the wrongdoer. Bad behavior, bad person.

Many theories of retribution rely not only on the belief that an injurer deserves punishment but also that the moral life is measurable. Therefore, each injury has a measurable compensation. Based on an ancient belief that injuries incur debts that must be paid, recompensed, this economic thinking explains why theories of retribution often assert that punishment is not only deserved, it must also be *in proportion* to the wrong. Proportionality can either be in kind (literally, an eye for an eye) or it can be symbolic, usually monetary. (The rabbis concluded that *lex talionis* had to be a metaphor, that the intention was surely to pay back in proportion to the injury.) In addition to the language of desert, then, retribution theories are chock full of the language of proportionality. This is supposed to correct the excesses wrought by rage. Kant said that punishment should be proportional to the moral iniquity, the act and the motive, the "inner viciousness." In such thinking, punishment becomes even a principle of fairness.[4] Hegel said that criminals have a "right" to punishment, that it demonstrates that we respect them as responsible beings. Again, that respect is grounded on their ostensible freedom of will.

Proportional thinking about punishment is often coupled to an emphasis on "distribution." We have seen that in Aristotle's theory of retribution, the judge is the equalizer who takes something away from the injurer and gives it to the injured to equalize. But injury is not a "good" to be distributed or measured out in fair quantity. Incredibly enough, Aristotle—the master of categorization—seems to have made an enormous category mistake. For him, the distribution of harm works the same way as the distribution of goods. That is, he applied distributive justice to wrongs. Aristotle's hope, like Kant's, was that by spreading the injury around—making the victim into a victimizer and returning harm with harm—he could set the moral order aright. But punishment, which is justified here as correcting an imbalance, does not in fact correct harm. It only adds more harm. As Plato's Socrates forcefully maintained, injuries are harms to be avoided.[5] Period. Hence, *any* addition to injury (whether by a victim or a state) results only in further harm, not in the restoration of any order.

If the theory of retribution is based on the inchoate idea that one should be punished because it is "deserved," that he must "pay for" wrongdoing, this is easily countered by the conviction that no one "deserves" to have harm done to him. It is a bizarre idea of wrongdoing that imagines that "balancing" harm in any way *corrects* injury instead of doubling injuries. "An evil deed is not redeemed by an evil deed," cautioned Martin Luther King, Jr. For him, violence is immoral because it thrives on hatred rather than on love. He added: "Violence is impractical because it is a descending spiral ending in destruction for all. It is immoral because it seeks to humiliate the opponent rather than win his understanding. It seeks to annihilate rather than convert. Violence ends up defeating itself. It creates bitterness in the survivors and brutality in the destroyers." John Milton writes that "revenge, at first though sweet, bitter ere long back on itself recoils," expressing the observation that the punisher ultimately punishes himself. Again, this is anticipated by Plato: "It is never just to harm anyone," for our goal is to cultivate virtue and men "become worse in human virtue when they are harmed."[6] They become even worse in virtue when they *do* harm.

How can Plato's insight differ so markedly from the intuitions of so many who uphold retribution? His notion of justice neither imagines paying back harms nor protecting transactions. Instead, for him, the purpose of justice is to order the soul and the city so that they can achieve their highest aims. His central metaphor for improving the character of persons is improving their health. No physician would treat an injury with another injury. Unlike the model of a bad person who should be punished, he depicts a hurting person who needs help. Unlike the freely choosing agent who embraces evil and must be defeated by our good, he depicts someone misguided, unable to see the good clearly. Plato, unlike so many others in his day—and ours— does not buy into the idea that justice requires a concept of reciprocity. "Social health" is indeed a profound metaphor, comprehending the idea that when people inflict and receive pain, their health and the health of the social body is impaired. When we see inflicting harm as the product of illness, we can spend the considerable resources on healing that we now devote to punishing, and better address the ailing social health of our communal body.

But Aristotle gained far more influence: ever since Aristotle, most theorists of retribution imagine harm as measurable, endorsing the concept that payment should be in proportion to the crime and thinking of harm distributively. They also describe this distribution of harm as a principle of fairness. This has led to such remarkable theories as Richard Posner's *Economics of Justice*, which even assigns an economic value to rape.[7] What can possibly "repay" such an injury? But as the bizarre idea of paying for rape so forcefully demonstrates, injury is not a good to be measured in fair quantities and made equitable for the moral order to be restored. Injury is not a "good" to be distributed. Rather, injuring someone, inflicting harm on another, is a violation of the moral order; hence, duplicating it only makes the moral order doubly violated. Imagine raping the rapist.

Other arguments, more attentive to the consequences than the motives of retribution, focus on deterrence. Punishment—rather, fear of punishment—is supposed to be an important motivation for doing the right thing. The assumption is behavioral, that we can offer rewards and punishments, goads and checks, to regulate behavior. Hardly anyone accepts that this is effective, however, as the statistics show that even the most extreme, capital punishment, does not act as a deterrent. Furthermore, such a manipulative version of human nature does not embrace human dignity as its chief virtue. Even the most committed behaviorists have found that people respond better to encouragement than to punishment, so that children are now to be raised with affirmations, and withholding them is powerful enough to serve as a disciplining warning.

Efforts have been made to distinguish retribution from revenge. According to the philosopher Robert Nozick, retribution is done for a wrong, not an injury. Retribution sets a limit to punishment, whereas revenge is endless. Retribution involves satisfaction for justice being done, while the satisfaction of revenge is from hurting another. Retribution is governed by general standards while revenge is governed by private ones. Retribution is impersonal, with the agent having no personal tie to the injurer, while revenge is deeply personal.

Intentionality plays a key role in his understanding of retribution: Nozick describes the "complicated structure" of retribution, "wherein something intentionally is produced in another with the intention that he realize why it was produced and that he realize he was intended to realize all this."[8] But if the intention is for an intention to be understood as such, what retribution is doing above all is *communicating*—sending a message that is vital to be received. With punishment, this communication is done in an "unwelcome way." Here is the first glitch in his theory: if the goal of communication is to be understood, this "unwelcome way" is likely to defeat the success of the communication. Messages that are delivered with doing harm are very likely to be resisted.

Nozick also argues that in retribution, "someone is shown something by being presented it directly. If an act is wrong because of what it does to someone else, the most powerful way to show him what it does is to do the same to him." Here a more obvious problem with his thinking emerges, for such logic would play out in a way that is patently absurd: if one is maimed for life by a gunshot wound, the offender would also need to be maimed for life. If someone is robbed, the offender needs to be robbed. Again, doubling an offense in order to "directly" communicate does not teach anything: it only doubles harms (Plato's insight). Nozick asserts, "The hope of retributive matching punishment is that the wrongdoer will realize his act was wrong when someone shows him that it was wrong and means it."[9] But if this is how moral education is achieved—by demonstrations of wrongdoing—then we are all in serious trouble! As Nozick himself notes (without taking in the lesson), "Many child-batterers were themselves battered children; their defect is not ignorance of what it is like to be battered."

Finally, Nozick argues, "the wrongdoer has become disconnected from correct values, and the purpose of punishment is to 're-connect' him. It is not that this connection is a desired further effect of punishment: the act of retributive punishment itself effects this connection."[10] While his diagnosis of a disconnect makes some sense, his conclusion defies logic. When he is harmed in this way, the victimizer only receives a moralized version of the same injury he inflicted. To tell him that his injury was wrong but ours is right (because it is retributive) makes no cognitive or experiential sense. There is a good reason why we do not teach children not to bite by biting them. Harming cannot teach that it is wrong to harm.

Still, as Nozick astutely discerned, the close companion of retribution is revenge. The emotions associated with it are hatred and rage, and because these are notably difficult to control, retribution has a tendency to slide into vengeance. And vengeance is notably given to spiraling into further vengeance. The codes of vengeance that characterized feuding societies even instituted this spiral: an injury had to be "paid back with interest." Perhaps we should be more suspicious of the likeness of retribution to revenge, of the similarities between legal and illegal violence.

Forgiving

What is forgiveness? Most definitions are negative: it is *not* succumbing to resentment, vindictiveness, or the desire to punish. The Greek *aphesis* suggests letting go; the Latin *ignoscere* suggests not knowing or overlooking. Forgiveness has been described as a change in inner feeling more than an external action. This is defined as "the overcoming, on moral grounds, of the intense negative reactive attitudes that are quite naturally occasioned when one has been harmed by another."[11] The "vindictive passions" to be overcome include "resentment, anger, hatred, and the desire for revenge." But forgiveness is not always understood as overcoming resentment—sometimes forgiveness takes place *even as* we resent, as it does for the Renaissance thinker Montaigne.

He that through a naturall facilitie and genuine mildnesse should neglect or contemne injuries received, should no doubt performe a rare action, and worthy commendation; but he who being toucht and stung to the quicke with any wrong or offence received, should arme himself with reason against this furiously blind desire of revenge, and in the end after a great conflict yeeld himselfe master over it, should doutlesse doe much more.... The first should doe well, the other vertuously: the one action might be termed Goodnesse, the other Vertue.[12]

Similarly, for Shakespeare's Prospero, the "greater virtue" requires reason triumphing over anger, rather than simply responding to injury with stoic calm of mind.

Forgiveness also includes a positive meaning, derived from its Old English etymology of *forgiefan*: *giefan* (to give), and *for-* (completely), that is, extreme giving. In this sense, forgiveness suggests more than simply overcoming resentment or reasoning beyond a will to punish. Forgiveness adds the positive goal of restoration. What is given, granted, is acknowledgement of the wrongdoer's remorse. What is granted is the opportunity for restoration in a disrupted relationship. This is extreme giving.

Forgiveness is not a unilateral act. It involves two: it is one's response to another's apology. Nor is it an isolated act: it is part of a process that includes the acknowledgement of wrongdoing, remorse, and apology from the perpetrator and the response of recognition of those and forgiveness from the injured. Without such acknowledgment of wrongdoing and without such remorse, forgiveness would be an empty gesture. But with them, forgiveness is performative, that is, the very act of forgiveness not only *acknowledges* the restoration of the moral order, forgiveness itself *restores* the right moral order.[13]

Forgiveness—not revenge—occupies the front and center of the biblical traditions' response to wrongdoing, with different religious traditions offering different paths to that goal. In medieval Judaism, the wrongdoer's change of heart enabled a sincere apology—there were standards to discern this—and this change of heart was the precondition for forgiveness. Are there cases when a wrong is unforgivable? In the Jewish tradition, forgiveness is only impossible when a wrongdoer cannot or will not sincerely repent.

The tradition views forgiveness as comprised of two interrelated duties—the duty of the offender to seek forgiveness is primary and unconditional, while the duty to grant it is conditional upon the offender's having fulfilled his or her prior duty. Thus, one has an obligation to forgive only if the offender has sincerely repented and sought reconciliation. Where the individual involved is reticent to acknowledge the harm done, one has a further obligation to rebuke the sinner in order to prompt that person to repentance. On the other hand, one is not obliged to forgive if the person will not or cannot repent, for this entails overlooking or minimizing their sinful behavior. Apart from this condition, however, the duty to forgive is unlimited with respect to the offense committed. "God's willingness to forgive, while conditional upon the sinner's repentance, is unlimited with respect to the severity of the sin."[14] And that divine forgiveness is the model for human forgiveness.[15] This rabbinic tradition is echoed by Jesus: "If another disciple sins, you must rebuke the offender, and if there is repentance, you must forgive" (Luke 17:3).

In the Christian Middle Ages, the sacrament of penance offered a public testimony of restitution, after confession and contrition, and these were the prerequisites for forgiveness. The simple "telling of one's sins" does not suffice to obtain forgiveness. "Without sincere sorrow and purpose of amendment, confession avails nothing, the pronouncement of absolution is of no effect, and the guilt of the sinner is greater than before."[16] Historically, this sacrament of penance had been displaced by Protestants during the Reformation by a doctrine of free grace, an absolutely unconditional divine forgiveness. But to be more precise, these two understandings—(1) that some debt must be paid that was incurred by wrongdoing, even if only an acknowledgement of it, and (2) that all debts are cancelled, that forgiveness requires no preconditions—exist alongside each other throughout most of Christian thought. Even the New Testament has both senses, authorizing both interpretations. On the one hand, the language of debt has been tied to forgiveness, as in the parable of the unforgiving debtor (Matt: 18:23). Christ is often spoken of as "paying for" man's sins. On the other hand, in the spirit of Nehemiah 9:17, forgiveness is always available: "you are a God ready to forgive, gracious, and merciful." Jesus instructs his disciples that they must forgive, not seven, but seventy-seven times (Matt. 18:22). Biblical injunctions on neighbor love are joined to a strong emphasis on love as forgiveness. Broadly, while the Hebrew Bible explains that justice is giving to those in need (and this is endorsed in the New Testament), so the New Testament focuses on a specific need and the gift that addresses it: the need to be forgiven (and this is affirmed throughout the Hebrew Bible). God's love enables human love. As it says, God loved humanity first (1 John 4:10). The suggestion is that humans need divine love to love, that this love is not only giving but forgiving of human inadequacy. "Forgive us our trespasses as we forgive those who trespass against us."[17]

In radical cases, forgiveness is prior to apology—in Jewish thought, God the Father forgives and in Christian thought, Christ forgives, but even this divine forgiveness is not quite unilateral. The forgiveness is still in a dialogue with the apology. Only here, the recognition and apology come after rather than before, with the prior forgiveness prompting the recognition of wrongdoing and remorse.

In the biblical traditions, God is depicted not just as judging, condemning, and executing righteous wrath, but as forgiving. This may seem surprising, but divine justice is persistently joined to forgiveness: "The Lord, the Lord, a god compassionate and gracious, long-suffering, ever constant and true, maintaining constancy to thousands, forgiving iniquity, rebellion, and sin and not sweeping the guilty clean away" (Exod. 34:6–7). In biblical prophecy, the restoration of the very relationship between God and Israel is enabled by forgiveness: "'Return, faithless Israel,' says the Lord. 'I will not look on you in anger, for I am merciful'" (Jer. 3:12). In the following fascinating passage, God is both forgiver and forgiven, granting clemency and apologizing.

> How can I give you up, Ephraim,
> How surrender you, Israel?
>
> · · · · · · · · · · ·
>
> My heart is changed within me,
> My remorse kindles already.
> I will not let loose my fury,
> I will not turn round and destroy Ephraim.   (Hos. 11:8–9)

God has the "change of heart" that Israel should have, on behalf of her, and he has that remorse for even considering responding to her with fury.

The brief book of Jonah allegorically distills the portrayal of divine forgiveness. It opens with the divine judgment against Nineveh, the wickedest city on the earth and the capital of the evil empire that sent Israel into exile. God's initial response to their evil is to threaten them through a dire message sent by his prophet Jonah: "Go to Nineveh, the great city, and inform them that their wickedness has become known to me" (1:2). But then, in a witty parody of the prophets who vehemently denounce evil and proclaim punishment, the book of Jonah describes a very *unwilling* prophet who is sent to denounce the city and its inhabitants.[18] He does not merely object to his commission, he runs in the opposite direction—boarding a ship to Tarshish instead of Nineveh. Thereafter, ironies redound. The sailors are foreigners who do not worship Yahweh, but when a great storm comes up, they ask Jonah to call on his God (not theirs), and when they learn that he is trying to escape from his God ("who made the sea and the land"!) they themselves call upon Yahweh before they throw Jonah overboard; then, when the sea grows calm, they immediately offer sacrifices to Yahweh and pray to him. The foreign sailors are more pious than God's prophet.

The message of the Lord will not go undelivered. That prophetic message is comically explored when "Yahweh appointed that a great fish" should be there to swallow Jonah when he is thrown overboard and this fish transports him to the shores of Nineveh after all, where "The word of the Lord was addressed a second time to Jonah:'Up!' he said,'Go to Nineveh, the great city, and preach to them as I told you'"

(3:1). Jonah makes a day's journey into the city (it takes three days) and says (you can almost imagine a whisper in the outskirts), "in forty days Nineveh is going to be destroyed." Some warning.

When the biblical prophets warn ancient Israel urgently that it will be destroyed if it does not reform morally, they are not heeded, and their dire prophetic warnings—of exile and destruction, of defeat by Israel's enemies—become predictions. That devastation or prosperity will visit ancient Israel according to its moral standards is the prevailing "deuteronomistic" vision from Deuteronomy through 2 Kings. In this context of the conventional deaf ear to prophetic warnings, the wretched Nineveh's exaggerated responsiveness to the prophet Jonah's warnings comically (and improbably) depicts repentance as extending from the greatest to the least of its inhabitants: "And the people of Nineveh believed in God." So when a repentant King issues a proclamation for thoroughgoing repentance, we are invited to imagine penitent chickens: "Men and beasts, herds and flocks, are to taste nothing; they must not eat, they must not drink water. All are to put on sackcloth and ashes and call on God with all their might; and let everyone renounce his evil behavior and the wicked things he has done." God saw their efforts "and God relented; he did not inflict on them the disaster he threatened."

Several conclusions emerge. First, even the most unspeakably wicked city on earth can still reform. Secondly, repentance is the precondition for the divine pardoning of Nineveh. Thirdly, the reason God gives for accepting this repentance, for not destroying even the wickedest city, is that it is his creation. In this comic parody of strict retributive (prophetic) justice, divine forgiveness responds so readily to the repentance of Nineveh that the forgiveness almost seems to have prompted it. This is how divine forgiveness works in Aquinas: it prompts repentance, and that is the reason that God forgives man even before his repentance—while humans forgive one another after repentance.

Although Nineveh has repented and God forgiven, the drama of repentance and forgiveness is not over. The prophet Jonah is filled with righteous wrath, furious with this course of events. He is the portrait of the retributivist who wants the wrongdoers punished "because they deserve it." According to Jonah, God is too soft-hearted: "That was why I fled to Tarshish: I knew that you were a God of love and compassion, slow to anger, rich in graciousness, relenting from evil. So now, Yahweh, please take away my life for I may as well be dead as go on living." The retributivist Jonah cannot bear living in a world where the wicked are not punished. But God, confronting Jonah's will to punish the deserving, asks him a simple ethical question, twice: "are you right to be so angry" at my forgiveness? The question works in two ways: exposing Jonah's motive of anger—is it right to be angry?—and questioning the value of the response that anger prompts—is it right to punish? Then, God instructs Jonah through experience: God appoints a plant to grow to shade Jonah from the scorching heat and then kills it. Jonah's dismay prompts the divine lesson:

"You are only upset about a plant which cost you no labor, which you did not make grow, which sprouted in a night and has perished in a night. And am I not to feel sorry for Nineveh, the great city, in which there are more than a hundred and thirty thousand people who cannot tell their right hand from their left, to say nothing of all the animals?"   (Jonah 4:10–11)

The prophet craves destruction; the divine response stresses creation. Jonah, the son of Amittai, is, literally, the son of Truth, and Jonah does not want to be made a liar. His own name, Jonah, means dove, alluding to the Flood at the time of Noah, where the appearance of a dove signals the newly found dry land, a renewal of creation. There and here, the divine purpose is not wrathful obliteration for wrongdoing, but the survival of the creation, only possible by righting the moral order. Jonah's righteousness is wrong.

The Book of Jonah offers one answer to the question: what would be the response to wrongdoing that is watched over by love? But it narrates the divine response. What about a human response to wrongdoing that is informed by love? Leviticus is once again helpful: "You shall not hate your brother in your heart; you shall surely rebuke your neighbor, and not bear sin because of him. You shall not take vengeance, nor bear a grudge against your neighbor...but you shall love your neighbor as yourself" (Lev. 19:17–18). As we have seen, in Rabbinic Judaism, forgiveness is "closely related to another duty, one especially incumbent on the injured party, namely, to chastise the wrongdoer if that person is unaware of the wrong committed."

This encourages the wrongdoer to repent, and hence to improve his moral character, and it saves others from being subjected to a similar offense. But rebuking also places a significant role on forgiveness. It highlights the fact that the act of forgiveness that follows this rebuke is NOT designed to minimize the offense or worse, to make believe that it did not occur. Quite the opposite is the case. It is because the offense and its effects are very significant to the parties involved that forgiveness is called for.... Forgiveness is meant to call attention to the morally objectionable nature of the offense at the same time that it facilitates a bridging of the gap that this offense has created.[19]

A rebuke is meant to be restorative for the perpetrator who has gone astray from the principles regarded as just in the community, and restorative for the victim, who is thereafter not forced to sustain the insult of wrongdoing unrecognized. In not leaving the offense unrecognized, rebuke also restores justice for the community. Rebuke and forgiveness, rather than ignoring the culpability of the offender, are designed to make it explicit. Perhaps this embrace of rebuke is part of what makes comprehensible that otherwise incomprehensible command of Jesus: to love the enemy. Does a rebuke satisfy justice itself? It is more likely that, rather than satisfy a pre-given justice, as punishment purports to do by distributing harm, rebuke—perhaps like forgiveness—works to create justice. In the activity of rebuke, right and wrong are given expression and definition. Justice comes into being.

Maimonides understood rebuke, apology, and forgiveness as reconstituting an impaired social moral order. This is why he insisted on seeking forgiveness from the dead, to prevent a "standing injustice" as Dan Philpott astutely terms it, from prevailing.[20] Maimonides says that if we committed a sin against someone who died and have not asked their forgiveness we must assemble ten people, who stand for the community, and together go to their grave and say, "I have sinned against the Lord and this individual." An interpersonal offense implies a sin against God, or, in secular terms, against the moral order. This means no less than seeking forgiveness from someone is also seeking to repair the moral order.[21]

For the philosopher Emmanuel Levinas, justice itself must flow from charity and answer to charity, the true source of justice. Simply put, "Love must always watch over justice."[22] He rejects a simply negative justice, one that only limits violence. In that vein, critics often speak of the relative weakness of human rights law as stemming from this negative understanding of justice, one that protects against violence but fails to promote human flourishing. Instead, Levinas urges a positive vision of justice that springs from charity. His clearest enunciation follows: "Justice itself is born of charity [love]. They can seem alien when they are presented as successive stages; in reality, they are inseparable and simultaneous, unless one is on a desert island."[23] Only a condition of complete isolation can separate us from reciprocal giving and forgiving.

The understanding of justice born of charity/love is delineated forcefully in the Hebrew Bible, both negatively, for Amos speaks of punishing the Israelites for their failure to be responsible for the poor, for the widow, orphan, and stranger—their failure to extend charity—and positively, for Jeremiah speaks of forgiveness: "They have found pardon in the wilderness, | those who have survived the sword. | Israel is marching to his rest" (Jer. 31:1–2). God affirms his love:

"I have loved you with an everlasting love, so I am constant in my affection for you. I build you once more; you shall be rebuilt, virgin of Israel. Adorned once more, and with your tambourines, you will go out dancing gaily." (Jer. 31:3–4)

Let's look harder at the unconditional model of forgiveness, for as a response to injury, it seems such a radical departure from the economics of retribution. Again, instead of requiring the injurer to pay for their hurting, or instead of hurting them back for hurting, the idea of unconditional forgiveness is that the injurer is freely forgiven. Several contemporary philosophers, Vladimir Jankelevitch and Jacques Derrida among them, have stressed that for forgiveness to be truly forgiveness and not in some way compromised, it needs to be unconditional in this way: this includes not requiring the work of confession, contrition, or even apology—all of which they understand as kinds of payment for the wrongdoing, a bargain in which an apology or penance is paid for forgiveness, thereby sullying with an economic exaction the purity of free, gratuitous forgiveness.

But while they hold out for the purity of unconditional forgiveness, both Derrida and Jankelevitch (despites their differences) see it as impossible for humans. Perhaps God, as transcendent sovereign, could forgive all freely, but not humans. There are many biblical precedents, such as Micah 7:18–19:

Who is a God like you, pardoning iniquity and passing over the transgression of the remnant of His heritage? He does not retain His anger forever, because He delights in mercy. He will again have compassion on us, and will subdue our iniquities. You will cast all our sins into the depths of the sea.

So attractive is this notion of unmerited grace, so beautiful is the concept of mercy as gratuitously given, so compelling is this idea of unconditional forgiveness, that *even as* Derrida found it humanly impossible, he was induced to rethink what he means by "impossible." Maybe, he wrote, "the impossible is just what is beyond the conditions of possibility," therefore something we can think, aspire toward, correct our own forgiveness in light of, even if we cannot actualize.[24] Jankelevitch writes of the madness, not of revenge, as in Shakespeare, but the madness of forgiveness. For him, unconditional forgiveness is a forgiveness without reason: if it has a reason, then there was something forgivable about the transgression after all, so forgiveness was merited and not freely given. Absolute unconditional forgiveness must not lower the severity of the crime to forgive it; reason must not mitigate the injury and neither must the passage of time.

Derrida underscored what theologians have long noted about the biblical traditions: again, that an economics of forgiveness, one that makes forgiveness conditional upon some act by the perpetrator, has existed alongside an an-economic model of forgiveness wherein forgiveness is unconditional, an absolutely free gift to one who can do and does nothing to deserve it. He has voiced grave, and surely responsible suspicions of the economic model. One of the reasons he is so suspicious of conditional forgiveness is that he sees a veritable explosion of "scenes of repentance, confession, forgiveness or apology" in which "not only individual, but also entire communities, professional corporations, the representatives of ecclesial hierarchies, sovereigns and heads of state ask for 'forgiveness.'" He refers to the Japanese Prime Minister's public apology to the people of South Korea and China, the Truth and Reconciliation Commissions of Chile and South Africa, and Pope John Paul II's apology for the Roman Catholic Church's silence in the face of Nazi atrocities. He worries that these gestures may be only strategic ruses, political publicity that compromises the real meaning of real forgiveness.

For his part, Jankelevitch points to the problem of the victim: the most victimized are dead and how can they be apologized to? How can the dead forgive? Either apologizing for our ancestors' crimes or offering forgiveness on behalf of the dead victims (how dare anyone?) can also seem far more like a mere political gesture than a movement toward genuine restoration. Conditional forgiveness harbors other perils. Not only are the terribly victimized already dead, but the living speaking victims, when they do forgive, engage in an act of paternalism over the injurer. They arrogate to themselves the power to forgive, a kind of violence of sovereignty: who are they to hold the well-being of your conscience in their hands?

Is forgiveness, like so many of our models of justice, also infected with economic thinking, and so we are left only to imagine an impossible forgiveness? I don't think that is the only option. With due respect for the hazards of a conditional understanding of forgiveness, I am going to ultimately embrace it. If what we mean by forgiveness is a completely free gift—offered to the unforgivable, one that erases the effects of the injury in order to achieve restoration—I would suggest that this demand of free forgiveness may not only be impossible but perhaps undesirable. We would have a world in which perpetrators of injury learn nothing. In that world, how would we begin to understand what is good and what is not? In contrast, conditional forgiveness harbors an opportunity for the restoration of the broken relation between the victim and injurer, a restoration of the moral order, and that kind of restoration cannot just be unilateral. This, in turn, does not compromise the free gift of love, *its* unconditionality, for such love is both the motive of forgiveness and its end. Through forgiveness the order of love is being restored. But forgiveness differs from love in that an injury has broken the love relation, and so its restoration cannot be unilateral. Motivated by love, both injured and injurer much reach together toward repair, toward love.

What the Catholic Middle Ages did was exact conditions for that forgiveness from the injurer. Work had to be done. This work—confession, contrition, and penance—was not just the precondition of forgiveness, it was part of the process of the overall labor of forgiveness. Ironically, despite Reformers' objections to "works" instead of faith, the term "work" is well-designated because the restitution of the moral order, the restoring of a broken relationship, the redirecting away of the will from the wrong objects of desire to the right ones, is indeed a labor, a huge labor. Perhaps forgiveness is a bigger labor even than mourning. At its best, this labor is shared by the church and by all social institutions, including the law, which can be not only be a punitive institution but a healing one.

To think this, it is important to distinguish the economics of punishment from that of forgiveness. The object exchanged is, after all, quite different: in one case, harm, in the other good, in one case unilateral willing of injury, in another, reciprocal willing of repair. Furthermore, "You can't owe forgiveness as an agent or earn it as a recipient in the standard senses of 'owe' and 'earn'...so forgiveness is beyond all appraisive questions of merit or desert or contract."[25] Forgiveness is relational, between someone who harms and someone harmed; and because their relation is broken, initiatives and responses are required from both for their relation to heal. Let me depict this, first as communication, but then, as narrative. From the side of the injured issues recognition of offense and rebuke, from the injurer, acknowledgement and confession, from the injured, an offering of help, from the injurer, remorse, from the injured, recognition of that remorse, from the injurer apology, from the injured, forgiveness. Forgiveness is a process, work that requires teamwork.

The Joseph Story

A remarkable biblical narrative offers further insight into the process of how rebuke, confession, acknowledgement, apology, and forgiveness engender justice: the story of Joseph in the book of Genesis. Joseph's brothers, envious of his special standing with his father and of his ambitions, throw him into a pit intending to murder him. But, unbeknownst to them, he survives, is sold into Egypt by traders passing by, and even prospers there. He becomes Pharaoh's right-hand man, his vizier, and saves all of Egypt from a devastating famine through his prudent agrarian policy. Later, one day Joseph finds himself confronting his once-scheming brothers. They have travelled from their famine-ridden home of Israel to Egypt to ask for food, and they fail to recognize, in the official before them, the brother they had tried to murder. What ensues is not simply punishment, nor ready, freely given forgiveness, but a severe rebuke as part of an agonizingly prolonged recognition scene. Joseph begins by speaking harshly to his brothers, accusing them of being spies, holding them in custody, but then gives them grain and puts money in their sacks. He demands that the brothers seeking food go back home and return with their adored youngest brother, and then, when they do, he demands that they leave him as a hostage, in exchange for grain. He is thereby requiring them to give away another brother, the one now most beloved by their father. He is inducing a repetition of their crime. At this,

They said to one another, "Truly we are being called to account for our brother. We saw his misery of soul when he begged our mercy, but we did not listen to him, and now this misery has come home to us... *They did not know that Joseph understood, because there was an interpreter between them*. He left them and wept. Then he went back to them and spoke to them. Of their number he took Simeon and had him bound while they looked on. (Gen. 42:21–4, my italics)

In this extraordinary scene, Joseph is simultaneously suffering and inflicting pain—leaving to weep and binding Simeon as a prisoner before his brothers' eyes. By means of this re-enactment, Joseph is trying to bring their earlier crime of abandoning another brother to their attention. Through this displacement, he succeeds in evoking a confession they do not know they are giving, for with an interpreter present, they have no idea that Joseph understands them. Their remorse is witnessed secretly and indirectly, and because "there was an interpreter between them," their external and internal remorse is harmonized; the figure of the translator enables the truth to appear.

The rebuke is prolonged and multi-faceted: next, Joseph plants a silver cup in the favored youngest brother's sack and accuses him of thievery. Now the very life of Joseph's brother Benjamin, the other child of the beloved Rachel, is imperiled. How do the once-murderous brothers respond to the threat posed to *this* favorite? One of the very ringleaders who had abandoned Joseph rises to the eloquent defense of his brother Benjamin. Judah responds,

Your servant our father said to us, "you know that my wife bore me two children. When one left me, I said that he must have been torn to pieces. And I have not seen him to this day. If you take this one from me too and any harm comes to him, you will send me down to Sheol with my white head bowed in misery." If I go to your servant my father now, and we have not the boy with us, he will die as soon as he sees the boy is not with us, for his heart is bound up with him. (Gen. 44:23–30)

Judah then offers himself as hostage in place of the loved boy. All of the violence and jealousy that the brothers had for the favored Joseph has now been transformed.

Upon Judah's acknowledgement of his proper responsibility, Joseph finally reveals his identity to his shocked brothers. They rebuke themselves for their wrongdoing, apologize, and he forgives them: "I am your brother Joseph whom you sold into Egypt. But now, do not grieve, do not reproach yourselves for having sold me here, since God sent me before you to preserve your lives" (Gen. 45:5–6). As in the book of Jonah, forgiveness is life-preserving.

Joseph's rebuke of his brothers, however harsh, is ultimately depicted as an act of love. Rather than punish for crimes and thereby redouble the violence, and rather than forget the offenses and thereby endanger the future of the moral order, rebuke—not only private but also public rebuke—awakens consciences.

It is because Joseph has retold his own story, albeit using substitutions, that he is able to revisit his injury, grieve, inspire confession and repentance, and finally, only then, forgive. The twelve tribes are thereby able to become the beginning of a nation, the nation designated to be a light to the nations. While the story he creates revisits the past, it triumphs over the helplessness that the past cannot be undone and the fear that the passage of time will lessen the severity of the crime. The time of narrative becomes the friend, not the enemy of injury because it is not the instant that, quickly passing, renders one unable to act, nor the time of forgetting, of erasure. The time of narrative can be the time of injurers trying, if not always succeeding, to move toward moral healing, and of the injured, trying if not always succeeding, to move toward forgiving, of humanity trying, but not always succeeding, to reconcile.

Hamlet: An Anti-Revenge Tragedy

In *Hamlet*, Shakespeare has written a sustained rumination on the problem of revenge, and it is no endorsement. The Ghost's request that the young Hamlet avenge his father's murder issues in a blood bath, leaving the stage strewn with bodies in the end. Unlike Thomas Kyd's *Spanish Tragedy*, where revenge is imagined as satisfying justice, the rottenness in the state of Denmark is not righted. Instead, violence spreads like a contagion, and the guiltless die with the guilty. This was noted forcefully in the eighteenth century when Samuel Johnson wrote:

The poet is accused of having shown little regard to poetical justice, and may be charged with equal neglect of poetical probability. The apparition left the regions of the dead to little purpose; the revenge which he demands is not obtained but by the death of him that was required to take it; and the gratification which would arise from the destruction of an usurper and a murderer, is abated by the untimely death of Ophelia.[26]

For Johnson, the ending of *Hamlet* is both improbable and unjust.

In the final act of *Hamlet*, the poisoned sword intended for Hamlet wounds Laertes; the poisoned cup intended for Hamlet kills his mother; and when Hamlet uses those instruments to kill Claudius, we are left feeling that the original command to avenge his father is only carried out circumstantially. It does not feel like revenge offers a just punishment to an injurer, but instead that it works haphazardly, wielding a clumsy sword that cuts down the innocent with the guilty. Hamlet kills Polonius unintentionally. Gertrude dies accidentally. The unjust deaths of Ophelia and Laertes seem like collateral damage. In this way, the causes and effects of revenge are disjoined, and the persons involved are substituted. After all, the parties to the injury are changed— the young Hamlet is not the elder murdered Hamlet. Revenge cannot correct an injury. Injuries are only compounded, often unintentionally—to Ophelia, Polonius, Laertes, Gertrude, and Hamlet. "Revenge, though sweet, bitter upon itself soon recoils." Shakespeare persistently depicts a ruined moral order as madness. Sanity requires not just reason, but the "right reason" of thinking justly, of living justly. In that context, revenge becomes a form of madness—not so much the calculated feigned madness that Hamlet dons, but the rage that, seizing Hamlet, distorts his love for Ophelia, leads him to kill the guiltless Polonius, and ultimately destroys his engagement with the world.

HORATIO   . . . give order that these bodies
   High on a stage be placed to the view;
   And let me speak to th' yet unknowing world
   How these things came about. So shall you hear
   Of carnal, bloody, and unnatural acts,
   Of *accidental* judgements, *casual* slaughters,
   Of deaths put on by cunning and for *no cause*,
   And in this upshot *purposes mistook*
   Fallen on th' inventors' heads: All this can I
   Truly deliver.   (5.2.361–9, italics added)[27]

Hamlet's famous hesitation does not only suggest his uncertainty about the truth of the crime; it also reflects uncertainty about a deeper truth, about the uncertainty of revenge as a valid moral code. And in the end, *Hamlet*, the greatest revenge tragedy in English drama, is an anti-revenge tragedy.

Throughout, the play underscores the enormity of the burden of revenge, the senselessness of the violence, and the impossibility of correcting injustice retributively. The crime—that Hamlet's father was murdered by his brother—*cannot* be righted. A passion for justice suggests that life has purpose and meaning. But the impossible demand made to Hamlet to correct the past, in the form of the request to avenge, inspires no such passion for a just order—only futility.

Over and over, the play stresses the temporal context of Eternity. The ghost comes from beyond the grave to seek revenge. Hamlet would kill himself, but the torments he imagines of an afterlife stop him. Gertrude must not be punished by Hamlet but by Heaven. The fate of Ophelia's body and soul is at risk due to her unlawful suicide, requiring that her death be mercifully interpreted as an accident in order for her to have a Christian burial. Hamlet himself says repeatedly that the dead are the lucky ones and in the end, his soul is wished to heaven: "Goodnight, sweet Prince, may flights of angels sing thee to thy rest." The yawning of an immeasurable time, then, is the context for both crime and punishment.

In such eternal time, neither the deed nor the retribution can be comprehended within the living duration of justice. Instead, injuries and their rectification become a passing shadow. The graveyard scene performs this message: in it, the imperial greatness of Alexander has become dust to stuff up a bunghole. Gazing at the skull of "poor Yorick," the jester who has now lost his laughter, Hamlet reflects that his mother could put an inch of paint on her face and still end up a bare skull.

Alas, poor Yorick. I knew him, Horatio. A fellow of infinite jest, of most excellent fancy. He hath bore me on his back a thousand times... Here hung those lips that I have kissed I know not how oft. Where be your gibes now—your gambols? your songs? your flashes of merriment, that were wont to set the table on a roar? Not one now, to mock your own grinning, quite chap-fallen. Now get you to my lady's table, and tell her, let her paint an inch thick, to this favour she must come. Make her laugh at that.   (5.1.174–84)

Her vain dissembling will be undone as surely as the merry jests of the clown. *Mutatus mundi*. The great and the mean, the righteous and criminal, the generous and the miserly, the good and the evil, are all leveled.

As he ruminates on the skull of a lawyer, Hamlet exposes the impotence of legal justice in the context of eternity.

HAMLET   There's another! Why, may not that be the skull of a lawyer? Where be his quiddities now—his quillets, his cases, his tenures, and his tricks?

> Why does he suffer this mad knave now to knock him about the sconce with a dirty shovel, and will not tell him of his action of battery? Hum! This fellow might be in's time a great buyer of land, with his statutes, his recognizances, his fines, his double vouchers, his recoveries. To have his fine pate full of fine dirt!   (5.1.93–101)

Echoes of the injustice of Hamlet losing his inheritance abound, with allusions to all of the means of securing the transfer of land, and inheritance—"conveyances, vouchers and double vouchers, recoveries."[28] All of the deeds that secure land transfer could scarcely fit in the coffin, and yet, in the end, the lawyer, who has taken possession of rather than inherited his lands, has, after all his cunning, no more land than his grave.[29]

> Will vouchers vouch him no more of his purchases and doubles than the length and breadth of a pair of indentures? The very conveyances of his lands will hardly lie in this box, and must th' inheritor himself have no more, ha? (5.1.93–105)

Death renders the legalities of justice futile.

Not only eternity, but the moment, the present instant, the "now" also haunts the play, doubling the futility of revenge. The moment, once past, cannot be revisited; events that happen now can neither be anticipated nor changed. What is done cannot be un-done and re-done. "If it be now, 'tis not to come. If it be not to come, it will be now. If it be not now, yet it will come." These lines are often plausibly interpreted as referring to the moment of death—for Horatio is here worried about Hamlet accepting a duel with Laertes. But surely they have a wider range of meaning (5.2.199). Once any event occurs it is not "to come." And if it is not in the future, it is now. The ghost who visits from the *afterlife* impossibly insists on Hamlet addressing the now:

> Now, Hamlet, hear:
> 'Tis given out that, sleeping in my orchard,
> A serpent stung me.
>
> .   .   .   .
>
>   But know, thou noble youth,
> The serpent that did sting thy father's life
> *Now* wears his crown.   (1.1.34–9)

Hamlet contemplates doing the bloody deed, intoning "now."

HAMLET   Tis *now* the very witching time of night,
    When churchyards yawn and hell itself breaks out

Contagion to this world. Now could I drink hot blood
And do such business as the day
Would quake to look on. Soft, *now* to my mother.   (3.2.378–82, italics added)

The bitter Day is the Judgement Day, so "now" is once again implicated with eternity.

Hamlet no sooner speaks of his bloodthirstiness, of drinking hot
blood, than his thoughts turn to chastising his mother, but as he heads
toward her room, he encounters Claudius at prayer. He works himself
up to using his dagger, intones the impossible *now*, but eternity disarms
him.

HAMLET   *Now* might I do it. But *now* 'a is a-praying;
  And *now* I'll do't. [*Draws sword*] —and so 'a goes to heaven;
  And so am I revenged. That would be scanned:
  A villain kills my father; and for that,
  I, his sole son, do this same villain send
  To heaven.
  Why, this is base and silly, not revenge.   (3.3.73–9, italics added)

Hamlet recoils at the summary of his own plot: killing Claudius now, at
prayer, would mean granting him eternity, in heaven. But then we learn
that the King's prayers were hollow, so that now Hamlet has missed his
chance. The moment passes, eternity mocks Hamlet's present project.

Not only the impossible temporality of revenge is put under scrutiny, but also the mode: is it an act of physical violence or a verbal one?
How are physical and verbal acts of aggression different, how related?
Hamlet's vivid renditions of using his sword follow this aborted murder; but here, even as he has just put up his physical sword, his words
become lethal daggers:

  No.
  Up sword; and know thou a more horrid hent
  When he is drunk, asleep or in his rage,
  Or in th'incestuous pleasure of his bed,
  At game a-swearing, or about some act
  That has no relish of salvation in't.
  Then trip him that his heels may kick at heaven
  And that his soul may be as damn'd and black
  As hell, whereto it goes. My mother stays;
  This physic but prolongs thy sickly days.   (3.3.87–96)

Hamlet tries to mete out eternal justice with that imagined sword: his
victim's heels kicking at heaven and his soul damned to hell. The blood

thirst continues, unsatisfied, as his thoughts return to his mother. But here, despite his resolve to use words and not daggers, his mother picks up the real danger. He only forces her to look into a glass to see herself and she responds fearfully that he is trying to murder her:

HAMLET   Come, come, and sit you down. You shall not budge.
  You go not till I set you up a glass
  Where you may see the inmost part of you.
QUEEN GERTRUDE   What wilt thou do? thou wilt not murder me—
  Help, ho!   (3.4.17–21)

How quickly deeds become words and words are taken for deeds is manifest in the shocking events that follow:

LORD POLONIUS   [*Behind*] What, ho! help, help, help!
HAMLET   [*Drawing*] How now! a rat? Dead, for a ducat, dead!
  [*Makes a pass through the arras*]
QUEEN GERTRUDE   O, what a rash and bloody *deed* is this!
HAMLET   A bloody deed! almost as bad, good mother,
  As kill a king, and marry with his brother.
QUEEN GERTRUDE   As kill a king!
HAMLET   Ay, lady, 'twas my *word*.   (3.4.22–8, italics added)

Hamlet has ostensibly come to speak to his mother, dagger in hand, and finds an excuse to use his weapon—almost, but not quite, on her. Instead, he stabs at the arras blindly, killing the innocent. Then, he has just stabbed someone when he says, "ay, 'twas my *word*." The distinction between words and wounds is made often in the play and as frequently collapses. This is because in *Hamlet*, words don't just represent blows; words strike blows.

> O heart, lose not thy nature. Let not ever
> The soul of Nero enter this firm bosom—
> Let me be cruel, not unnatural:
> I will speak daggers to her, but use none.
> My tongue and soul in this be hypocrites.
> How in my words somever she be shent,
> To give them seals never my soul consent!   (3.2.383–9)

"Speaking daggers" suggests that words can wound. The anxious distinction the children's nursery rhyme tries to make—"Sticks and stones can break my bones but words can never hurt me"—belies how deeply wounding words can truly be.

The daggers of Hamlet's words do sink deep into his mother, "O Hamlet thou hast cleft my heart in twain!" No physical violence against your mother, advised the Ghost, let the violence of thorns in her bosom prick and sting her. But here, we have a hint that the violence of words harbors a force different from physical violence. In a play where daggers stab randomly through an arras, perhaps the daggers of words, the thorns and pricks of conscience, have some stronger moral force.

During his sustained rebuke of his mother, Hamlet proceeds to make the distinction between Gertrude's worthless physical response of wringing her hands and the moral response he seeks with his violent words:

> Leave wringing of your hands. Peace! sit you down
> And let me wring your heart. For so I shall,
> If it be made of penetrable stuff,
> If damned custom have not brazed it so
> That it is proof and bulwark against sense. (3.4.32–6)

If her heart is not hardened, "brazed" against feeling, then Hamlet will wring her heart. This image of astonishing violence is not meant to crush her heart, but to repair it, not to destroy her but to enable a change of heart.

In the midst of this profound critique of revenge, then, something else is offered: *rebuke*. The Ghost has forbidden Hamlet from harming his mother, leaving her punishment to God and to her conscience. Hamlet is thereby expressly forbidden the classical path, the one Orestes takes in Aeschylus' trilogy, killing his mother to avenge his father's murder, or the path of Nero, who had his mother Agrippina murdered for poisoning her husband and living with her brother.

> GHOST   If thou hast nature in thee bear it not,
> Let not the royal bed of Denmark be
> A couch for luxury and damned incest.
> But howsomever thou pursues this act
> Taint not thy mind nor let they soul contrive
> Against thy mother aught; leave her to heaven
> And to those thorns that in her bosom lodge
> To prick and sting her. (1.5.81–8)

But while Hamlet may leave his mother's punishment to heaven, he does take her moral education upon himself. He deliberately substitutes his rebuke ("shent" is the past participle of the archaic verb "shend," to rebuke or scold) for blood-letting. Instead of stabbing her, he wrings her heart. And in this anti-revenge play where daggers are futile, rebuke is not futile.

The passage in the Bible that enjoins us to love the neighbor as ourselves also says you shall not take vengeance against him and further, that you shall not bear a grudge against him. Even vindictive feelings are anathema: "You shall not hate your brother in your heart; you shall surely rebuke your neighbor, and not bear sin because of him. You shall not take vengeance, nor bear a grudge against your neighbor... but you shall love your neighbor as yourself" (Lev. 19:17–18). The injunctions against vengeance, against hating, and even against bearing a grudge, all alongside the command to love the neighbor, have a notably odd companion, one that seems to not fit: "You shall surely rebuke your neighbor." Why?

The Jewish philosopher Maimonides offers an answer, and does so in the context of commenting upon the love command of Leviticus:

When a man sins against another, the injured party should not hate the offender and keep silent... his duty is to inform the offender and say to him, "Why did you do this to me? Why did you sin against me in this matter?" And thus it is said, "You shall surely rebuke your neighbor" (Lev. 19:17). If one observes that a person committed a sin or walks in a way that is not good, *it is a duty to bring the erring man back to the right path* and point out to him that he is wronging himself by his evil courses... If the offender repents and pleads for forgiveness, he should be forgiven.[30]

This idea of rebuke sounds foreign to modern ears. It can either suggest a version of social policing—images of Calvin's Geneva come to mind—or an ineffectual response to wrongdoing, one soft on crime. How can a rebuke really stop an offender? Moreover, how can one possibly intervene to offer correction without infringing upon another's rights? "Coercion for a person's own good or coercion for the perceived general long range moral good of society is in most cases to be ruled out" of our legal codes.[31] Indeed, interfering with someone can only be justified in the most extreme cases.[32] Whatever rebuke is, it is another way, a third way: neither retribution, nor forgetting the crime.

The distinction I have sought to complicate between wounds and words takes me back to Hamlet's own critique of mere words. He rages against their uselessness when he craves committing physical harm.

> Why, what an ass am I: this is most brave,
> That I, the son of a dear murdered,
> Prompted to my revenge by heaven and hell,
> Must like a whore unpack my heart with words,
> And fall a-cursing, like a very drab,
> A stallion! Fie upon't, foh! About, my brains!   (2.2.517–22)

All his talk of words' insufficiency leads him to what? Not to action, but to conclude that a *play* is exactly what he needs. Witnessing a play, one can be struck to the soul (this language of physical wounding is familiar), so struck that he proclaims his wrongdoing. Hamlet tells us that a play can function as a rebuke, prompting confession.

> I have heard
> That guilty creatures sitting at a play
> Have by the very cunning of the scene
> Been struck so to the soul that presently
> They have proclaimed their malefactions;
> For murder, though it have no tongue, will speak
> With most miraculous organ. I'll have these players
> Play something like the murder of my father
> Before mine uncle.   (2.2.523–31)

Hamlet also stages his rebuke of his mother theatrically, holding up mirrors and portraits. It may not be too much to suggest that the play stages a theater of rebuke, not retribution, showing misdeeds, holding up that mirror of nature, to prompt an ethical response in its audience.

Such moral rebuke, as part of a process of communication and restoration of relationship, is not just the purview of theater, of course, but also of narrative more broadly understood—including psychoanalytic narrative, journalistic narrative, the narratives of history, the narratives of literature, the narratives we tell ourselves and others, even in social conversation. When injuries are revisited and retold, the work can be done of seeing when the wrong object was sought and of reframing that error within the quest for the good, of re-contextualizing. In this process the original experience of injury is not denied, not forgotten, not covered over, nor is it re-done, but it can be re-crafted into a new understanding that could culminate in the possibility of forgiveness, which, as the philosopher Hannah Arendt said, frees us for a new act, freed of the consequences of the old injury.[33] In this process, the injured "re-discovers the love for his own and the others' real good, which essentially motivated [what was once his hatred] and sees that what was really hated was the negative impairment of love and the good."[34] In another words, forgiveness frees the injured for a new narrative. The wounding words of theater cannot undo the crimes of humanity, cannot fix them, but they can wring our hearts.

After all, it is not so surprising that *Hamlet* does not endorse revenge.[35] The play reflects an Elizabethan Christian ethos that makes revenge not only unsavory, but sinful. "The primary argument against revenge . . . was that the revenger endangered his own soul. No matter how righteous a man might think his motives, the act of revenge would inevitably make him as evil as his injurer in the eyes of God," explains one scholar.[36] A sermon summarizes well: "In so going about to revenge evill, we shew our selves to be evill, and, while we will punish, and revenge another mans folly, we double, and augment our owne folly."[37] The Christian anti-revenge code had such widespread influence that "the average spectator at a revenge play was caught in an ethical dilemma—a dilemma, to put it most simply, between what he believed and what he felt."[38] Presumably, he felt the urge for vengeance even as he condemned it.

We need not assume that theatrical productions only *reflected* an already forged ethos against revenge. Rather, we have every reason to believe that a popular drama like *Hamlet* helped to forge it. *Hamlet* is not an isolated instance: throughout the corpus of Shakespeare, revenge is suspect. In *Romeo and Juliet*, the code of vengeance destroys the young lovers.[39] In *Troilus and Cressida*, revenge "is the nurse of barbarism and irrational frenzy."[40] In *Othello*, Shakespeare provocatively joins the urge to revenge to madness. When Othello's delusion deepens into madness, he spews out this perverse vow: "Arise, black vengeance, from the hollow hell! | Yield up, O love, they crown and hearted throne | To tyrannous hate!" (3.3.447–9). And in *King Lear*, as in *Othello*, the onset of Lear's madness coincides with his vow of vengeance. Lear begins by praying for patience toward his unkind daughters, but soon gives himself up to rage, and to madness:

> No, you unnatural hags
> I will have such revenges on you both,
> That all the world shall—I will do such things—
> What they are, yet I know not; but they shall be
> The terrors of the earth.   (2.4.281–5)

Many of Shakespeare's plays not only condemn revenge. They endorse forgiveness, even—especially—when one is seized by fury.

> Though with their high wrongs I am struck to the quick,
> Yet with my nobler reason 'gainst my fury
> Do I take part: the rarer action is
> In virtue than in vengeance. (*The Tempest*, 5.1.25–8)

Furthermore, forgiveness is not only offered as an alternative to revenge. It holds much more: forgiveness is tied to recognition, the rediscovery of love.[41] For one critic, recognition virtually constitutes Shakespeare's gospel: "The Good News that Shakespeare's last plays bring to us is that we can reach happiness on earth, and that this can be true 'eternal life.' To be reunited with one's loved ones, to rediscover them and recognize them, constitutes happiness: nothing more than this, but equally nothing less."[42] We have seen that such acknowledgement reaches exquisite intensity in the recognition scene between Lear and Cordelia when he awakens from his madness, and the disinherited Cordelia asks for Lear's blessing as the penitent Lear begs her forgiveness:

CORDELIA   O! Look upon me, Sir,
  And hold your hand in benediction o'er me.
  No, Sir, you must not kneel. (4.7.58–60)

Piero Boitani comments:

"Forget and forgive," Lear will shortly implore. Recognition thus means, in the instant between past, present, and future, a new awareness, an opening of the mind towards the other, which contrasts with Lear's previous falling in on himself. That earlier kind of knowledge was the all-too-human wisdom of madness: this present knowledge, which is forged by the earlier one through a wheel of fire, is communion; it is a fully human wisdom sublimed and purified by acceptance.[43]

Shakespeare's understanding of justice flows not only from classical conventions but also from the biblical tradition, where forgiveness enables just restorations of an injured social order, where love is bound to justice. Even in his romantic comedies like *As You Like It* or *Twelfth Night*, what satisfies is the disentanglement of the wrong partners and the mutual recognition of the right ones: the *ordo amoris*, the order of love, including the marital order, must be right for the social order to be just. What constitutes a "tragedy" is not only its conclusion in dead bodies, but the triumph of injustice. With the murders of Desdemona and Cordelia, not only are innocent people destroyed, but goodness, even love, seem defeated. That this defeat registers as so tragic signals, perhaps better than its victory, that the play offers an ethos of justice as love.

The "play within the play" conventions in *Hamlet,* the substitutions in the Joseph narrative, and the puppetry in Jonah are no accident. Distancing and indirection enable the kind of admissions and confessions that restore the moral order. The murder of Gonzago, not Hamlet, stirs the conscience of Claudius. The capture of Benjamin, not Joseph, stirs the conscience of Judah. The very substitutions that make the project of revenge fail enable the project of forgiveness to succeed. This includes temporality, for the same phenomenon of the passing of time that prevents any injury from genuinely being rectified by revenge enables the reflection of conscience. Looking back, Lear and Judah can apprehend their wrongdoing and looking back, Joseph can pause and not act on the immediate urge to revenge. God's rebuke of Nineveh, Joseph's rebuke of his brothers, Hamlet's rebuke of his mother, the rabbinic embrace of rebuke, and the Church's sacrament of penance harbor potential for reconciliation, for the symbolic exchanges that take place both in narrative and in ritual are not "mere" symbols; they model the hard work of forgiveness, which in a world of ongoing trespass, is our social glue.

Like so many of Shakespeare's plays, *The Tempest* is also preoccupied with injury and forgiveness.[44] The background is another heinous injustice. As Joseph's jealous brothers abandoned him to die in a pit, so, in *The Tempest,* Prospero's brother has abandoned Prospero and his young daughter to die at sea, usurping his throne. More plots ensue of treachery and betrayal: a plot to murder the King of Naples by his brother, and a plot to murder Prospero and take over the island by Caliban, Stephano, and Trinculo. Prospero must not only abort the new treachery and right the old wrongs, he must also dispense justice. Notably, this is imagined in the play not as the work of the public court or of private feuding, but as the creative work of the theater. Prospero is the master artist who creates a world through his vision and the magic of conjuring, i.e. theater. That made world will be made just.

Once the villains are in Prospero's power, he is tempted to punish his brother Alonso for his misdeeds—"bountiful fortune | (Now, my dear lady) hath mine enemies | Brought to this shore" (1.2.178–80);

"At this hour | Lies at my mercy all my enemies" (4.1.263–4). But instead he creates the conditions that will inspire his enemy to experience remorse: he induces Alonso to believe that he has lost his own son in the tempest. It works: Alonso interprets his devastating loss as the payment for his own dreadful crime of casting Prospero and his daughter out to sea.

ALONSO   O, it is monstrous, monstrous!
   Methought the billows spoke and told me of it;
   The winds did sing it to me, and the thunder—
   That deep and dreadful organpipe—pronounced
   The name of Prosper. It did bass my trespass.
   Therefore my son i'th'ooze is bedded, and
   I'll seek him deeper than e'er plummet sounded,
   And with him there lie mudded.   (3.3.95–102)

Miranda responds sympathetically to the suffering of Alonso and his companions in the tempest—"O I have suffered with those that I saw suffer" (1.2.5–6)—and even Prospero's sprite Ariel feels sympathy for those suffering. But Prospero, meting out justice, only recovers such sympathy when his victimizers have shown remorse. He seeks remorse, apology, and to correct the standing wrong—not vengeance.

   Hast thou, [Ariel] which art but air, a touch, a feeling
   Of their afflictions, and shall not myself
   (One of their kind, that relish all as sharply,
   Passion as they) be kindlier moved than thou art? . . .
        The rarer action is
   In virtue than in vengeance. They being penitent,
   The sole drift of my purpose doth extend
   Not a frown further.   (5.1.21–30)

Revenge is not Prospero's intention; justice is. His sole purpose is their penitence, not a frown further. Once that is achieved, Prospero forgives, and with that restoration, he is willing to abjure his staff, abdicate his godlike magic powers, and give up the need to conjure a just world (5.1.21–4).

Once again, the passing of time and substitutions of personae that make the project of revenge impossible enable the project of the restitution of the moral order. In the imagined unjust worlds inhabited by Hamlet, Jonah, Joseph, and Prospero, remarkably enough, moral lessons are taught and learned through fictions within those fictions. Plays are performed, dramas are orchestrated, personae are manipulated, magic

↓—all in the service of restoring justice. In all of these stories, ¿onist confronts the temptation of revenge, but in the end he ~~ ay toward a more creative solution, to staging dramas that induce recognition, apology, and (except in *Hamlet*) enable forgiveness. No direct confrontations, but indirection, substitutions—no immediate response, but delayed action—allow remorse and apology to grow unhampered by the defenses set in motion by personal accusation. In biblical narratives and in the biblical Shakespeare, then, rebuke is joined to forgiveness, justice to love.

We might well ask, why does legal discourse minimize the significance of forgiveness when religious discourse values it so highly? As we have seen, the law presumes not only the right but the duty to punish: it does not ask whether it should punish, but how much, who, when, and how. In the legal literature, there are four justifications for punishment:

- retribution: punishment is needed because it is deserved. This means only such punishment as is proportional to the harm. This concept of punishment includes repaying for some advantage someone has stolen.
- incapacitation: to keep the criminal from doing further harm. This includes both the specific (the harms that criminal could commit) and the general (the harms other potential criminals could inflict on society). The effort is to control dangerous anti-social conduct.
- expressive: punishment expresses the community's commitment to the norms that were violated.
- rehabilitation: the function of punishment is to teach, to educate.

The first justification is by far the one most frequently invoked: the paying back of a debt incurred by injury. Rehabilitation is regarded as costly and unduly generous. Impulses to rehabilitate have given way to a climate of retribution. Forgiveness is not even on the radar screen. How could our "corrective" system be more responsive to the moral value of forgiveness, one so strong in the western cultural imaginary?

In biblical traditions, desert seems to be swept away as a criterion for punishment. If God did not continually forgive his creation, there would be no creation. For Luther, if God punished all sinners, there would be no one left. Instead, forgiveness is the outpouring of love precisely to one who does not deserve it. Forgiveness, like love, exceeds desert. And in religious thought, human forgiveness is enjoined to imitate this exceeding forgiveness attributed to God.

Jesus engaged in a polemical attack on what Nicholas Wolterstorff calls "the reciprocity code," the assumption that good should be reciprocated with good and evil with evil. "Love your enemies, do good to those who hate you, bless those who curse you, pray for those who abuse you" (Luke 6:27–8).[45] His most radical formulation includes loving the enemy:

You have learned that they were told, "Eye for eye, tooth for tooth." But what I tell you is this: Do not set yourself against the man who wrongs you . . . You have heard that they were told "Love your neighbor, hate your enemy." But what I tell you is this: Love your enemy and pray for your persecutors: only so can you be children of your heavenly father, who makes the sun rise on the good and the bad alike, and sends the rain on the honest and dishonest. (Matt. 5:38–9 and 43–5)[46]

Why are these biblical teachings, carried forward so effectively in Shakespearean drama and embraced by generations of theater-goers (if not believers), left behind when we enter the halls of political and legal thought? The concept of the human person as worthy, as possessed with ineradicable dignity, as capable of caring, of loving, forges a completely different ethos than that flowing from the image of the competitive, brutish, warring human that dominates political thought. But surely, that anthropology of innate human violence is self-perpetuating. After all, those who harm are harming themselves. Conversely, the anthropology of loving humans can achieve, not only healing for the injured, but more: the radical gift of forgiveness.

Afterword

In closing, I want to return to the question of the neighbor. We are here a long way from the vision of a person presupposed by modern liberal thought. That self is imagined as a "separate, individual person, each with [his] own aims, interests, and conceptions of the good life ... freed from the sanctions of custom and tradition and inherited status, unbound by moral ties" and capable of steering his course with freedom—so that often what is most just is to "let him be." This is the language of negative rights. As Michael Sandel summarizes, "for the liberal self, what matters most is not the ends we choose but our capacity to choose them."[1]

In the older tradition we have seen our fellow man is someone who doesn't have enough, and so we must feed him, and someone who is away from home, and so we are obligated to reach out to him. What then does it mean to love such a fellowman? To respect him, indeed, but far more: to help him. This justice is not the same as fulfilling a contract, duty to the moral law, a calculus of utility, distributing equitably or in just proportion, nor retribution for an injury. Giving to those in need is not quite based on their desert, their merits, nor is it precisely the same as their right. What the fellow claims is not only his right, his freedom to possess his goods or pursue his ends without interference; what he also claims is my responsibility to care for him.

Here, I cannot help but contrast Shakespeare's Juliet to Bizet's Carmen. Carmen speaks the language of freedom: "la Liberté." Her freedom must be protected—from law and from love, at all costs. This is her priority. Nothing, no consideration can take priority over that right. The right trumps the good and the right in question is freedom. Carmen is often heralded as the first feminist but may be better understood as one of the first modern liberal subjects, willing to die for her freedom. But the question that thoughtful philosophers pose to defenders of liberalism is the one Carmen raises: freedom for what? Is this freedom for its own sake, its own end? The opera also raises the corollary question: freedom from what?

Carmen's world is one of possessions, of gaining, losing, and stealing possessions. She steals Don Jose as a possession; she throws him away as a possession; and moves on to acquiring her next one. She has projected this image of possession onto everything in her world—will Don Jose be possessed by the army, by his mother, or by her? Within such a worldview, she emanates courage and conviction when she refuses to be stolen. But this vision is in perfect alignment with the understanding of the modern subject as possessor in a world of possessions and possessors whose right to possess is understood as her primary freedom. In this light, Carmen is the possessor of her own sexuality. She will put it to work in whatever way she chooses, deploy it to free herself from the law, to divert customs officers during thefts, to take whatever partner she wants and reject whomever she wants, to lure one man after another under her sexual spell. To the extent that she embraces the freedom to possess her own sexuality, Carmen seems heroic. But to the extent that this freedom is not *for* any notion of the good, but is only for its own sake, it is exposed as a dangerous game, even a perverse ideology to embrace.

If our model of the human person is not that of the individual bounded by his body, his soul, his conscience, his consciousness, but of a person embedded in a deep network of association from which he would cease to be if he were cut off from his past, his future, his present, as well as his neighbors, his strangers, then the unavoidable intertwining of others' well-being in his well-being and vice versa is the starting ground. Much of the fiction of liberal individualism—as self-sufficient, autonomous, with self-interested aims—gives rise to the anxiety of co-opting another's autonomous self-sufficient experience (or property). But from the lenses of love, the ethical challenge becomes not so much how to avoid co-opting another but to find the resources within and without to respond to another's need. Challenging the liberal fiction of freedom and the attachment to rights that guarantee freedom is a world of obligation, a web of human ties that envelop us, and that ask that we live ethically within that web.

The advances made by liberalism are impressive—its values of impartiality, utility, and measure are a leap forward from a world of private bonds infected by hatreds, prejudices, and injustice. Religious and ethnic minorities and women have suffered horrifically and without recourse before the new values of liberalism were put in place. But this book asks if by throwing away the value of affective bonds we have thrown away the baby with the bathwater, or, to mix metaphors, have we allowed the pendulum to swing too far from the bonds of affection to the neutrality of universal rights? Now that our sublime liberal values are in place, perhaps we can afford to admit to their shortcomings, and to put love back on the map of human justice.

I know that altruism often looks irrational. But this is because in most of our thinking about reason, the role of reason is to serve self-preservation and self-interest. When we say something is rational we usually mean it is self-interested. And this makes all acts and attitudes that are not self-interested "irrational." My law students thought Juliet made an irrational choice to remain devoted to her exiled lover instead of marrying the available County Paris, and that she was simply wacky to kill herself over Romeo. Many colleagues thought I was nutty to suspend my work to nurse my bedridden mother at home. And, as we have seen, because Freud understands the human person as fundamentally most interested in his own flourishing, the command to love the neighbor as oneself seems unreasonable to him: "Why should we do it? What good will it do us?" But when we redefine reason, as promoting the well-being not only of myself but the others I am inevitably bound to in the world, both those I encounter and those who are unknown to me, others whose flourishing is indeed implicated in my own, then "other-regarding behavior," that is, *giving*, is suddenly supremely sensible—maybe even rational.

Notes

CHAPTER I. THE EXPERIENCE OF LOVE

1. Notable exceptions are Raimond Gaita's *A Common Humanity: Thinking about Love and Truth and Justice* (London and New York: Routledge, 2000), Martha Nussbaum's *Political Emotions: Why Love Matters for Justice* (Cambridge: Harvard University Press, 2013; released, unfortunately, after this went to press), and Nicholas Wolterstorff's *Justice in Love* (Grand Rapids: Wm. B. Eerdmans, 2011).
2. This is the title of an excellent discussion by T. M. Scanlon, *What We Owe to Each Other* (Cambridge, MA: Harvard University Press, 2000).
3. Gaita, *Common Humanity*, 25.
4. Ibid. 26.
5. Ibid.
6. Another important contributor to our thought on the interdependence of Justice and Love is Nicholas Wolterstorff. See his *Justice in Love*.
7. Hobbes was more attentive to the emotions than many philosophers, even as he believed that humans were governed by "brutish" ones.
8. *Nicomachean Ethics*, 5.4 (1132a25–30), trans. W. D. Ross (Oxford: Clarendon Press, 2009).
9. For Aristotle, distribution is geometric, not arithmetic; by this he means that one thing is equivalent to another, even if it is not literally the same, even if it cannot be measured (for the misguided King Lear, as we will see, flattery seems equivalent to property). Rawls is embracing a more arithmetic distribution, in which the same thing is distributed equally, including equal opportunity.
10. Government may respect organizations and foundations that donate time, energy, and resources to righting injustices in the world, and that respect may translate—ironically enough—into a tax deduction for some (as money is the currency that runs the political sphere), but that does not mean that the political sphere has seriously integrated the lessons of religious thought on justice.
11. Chad Wellmon, "Kant and the Feelings of Reason," *Eighteenth-Century Studies*, 42/4 (Summer 2009), 557–80, 1.

12. *Metaphysics of Morals*, trans. and ed. Mary Gregor (Cambridge: Cambridge University Press, 1996), 161.

13. On equal opportunities see the important work of Martha Nussbaum and Amartya Sen.

14. Because modern translations of the Bible employ vocabulary more familiar to our ears, I have turned most often to the NIV Hebrew–English Old Testament (Grand Rapids, MI: Zondervan, 1979), quoted here, and to The Jerusalem Bible (London: Darton, Longman and Todd and Doubleday and Company, 1966). If Shakespeare's attention to the specific language of the Bible is at issue, I have cited the Geneva Bible (GVN), the one Shakespeare would have likely read. Occasionally, I have had recourse to the King James Bible (KJV) for its sheer poetry.

15. See rich discussions of the law in Bradin Cormack, Martha Nussbaum, and Richard Strier (eds), *Shakespeare and the Law: A Conversation among Disciplines and Professions* (Chicago: Chicago University Press, 2013); Bradin Cormack, *A Power to Do Justice: Jurisdiction, English Literature, and the Rise of Common Law, 1509–1625* (Chicago: Chicago University Press, 2008); Lorna Hutson, *The Invention of Suspicion: Law and Mimesis in Shakespeare and Renaissance Drama* (Oxford: Oxford University Press, 2011); Paul Kahn, *Law and Love: The Trials of King Lear* (New Haven: Yale University Press, 2000); Craig Muldrew, *The Economy of Obligation* (New York: St Martin's Press, 1998); Peter Goodrich, *Law in the Courts of Law: Literature and other Minor Jurisprudences* (New York: Routledge, 1996); Subha Mukerji, *Law and Representation in Early Modern Drama* (Cambridge: Cambridge University Press, 2009).

16. Hannibal Hamlin, *The Bible in Shakespeare* (Oxford: Oxford University Press, 2013) argues that there is specific language in *King Lear* directly attributable to the *Sermons*, pp. 312–14. The *Sermons* went through five editions in the decade after it was published (1574), and was adopted by several parishes for the use of parishioners.

17. Luther, *The Works of Martin Luther* (Philadelphia: Muhlenberg Press, 1930), 16, 22.

18. Ibid., "Secular Authority," trans. J. J. Schindel, III. 228–73; p. 272.

19. In *The Economy of Obligation*, Craig Muldrew has argued that in the early modern period, economic relations depended upon trust and a belief in neighbor love, as cash was not readily accessible, and credit involved assessments of integrity.

20. It is a risky enterprise to over-generalize about Shakespeare as his plays are so diverse. Exceptions to every rule can certainly be found. But in many of the tragedies, the notable absence of love leads to excesses of injustice, and in many of the comedies, the presence of love restores justice.

CHAPTER II. THE LAW OF LOVE

1. Alternatively, strains of Christianity have brought together the law and justice and separated both from love. See especially Anders Nygren, *Agape and Eros*, trans. Philip S. Watson (London: SPCK, 1953).

2. We find this endorsed in Maimonides, Hillel, Rashi, in Augustine, Aelred of Rievaulx, Bonaventura, Bernard of Clairvaux, Richard of St Victoire, Aquinas, on through to Pope Benedict.

3. Lenn Goodman, *On Justice: An Essay in Jewish Philosophy* (Oxford and Portland, OR: Littman Library of Jewish Civilization, 2008; 1st edn. Yale University Press, 1991), p. viii. Many thinkers want to conflate contract with covenant, seeing the covenant as a proto-contract. I find it more helpful to retain the more precise meaning of contract between two consenting partners of equal ability to enforce it. The force of the biblical covenant is identity constituting for the community; as I have described in *The Curse of Cain*, the people are hereafter the people of this God.

4. Nicholas Wolterstorff has offered the most persuasive account of rights theory as the claim others make upon us, that is, a rights theory that includes obligation. See his *Justice in Love*.

5. Goodman, *On Justice*, 6.

6. Immanuel Kant, *Grounding for the Metaphysics of Morals*, trans. James W. Ellington, 3rd edn. (1785; Indianapolis: Hackett Publishing Company, 1993), *Ak.* 399.

7. Sigmund Freud, *Civilization and its Discontents*, in *The Standard Edition of the Complete Psychological Works*, trans. and ed. James Strachey, Vol. 21 (1930; London: Hogarth Press, 1957–74), 109–12, 142–3.

8. In Nicholas Wolterstorff's *Justice in Love*, his understanding of justice as care is largely compatible with the vision of justice as giving that I am delineating in the Bible. He does include a place for one's worth making a claim on us beyond one's need: to treat someone as would only befit something of less worth is to treat them unjustly. To shift the emphasis to need is to shift it away from a theory presuming valuation.

9. This is elaborated in Schwartz, "Milton on Idolatry: *Samson Agonistes*," *Oxford Handbook of Milton*, ed. Nicholas McDowell and Nigel Smith (Oxford: Oxford University Press, 2009). One prominent Miltonist, John Carey, has deemed Samson as virtually a suicide bomber for tearing the Temple down on the Philistines in *Samson Agonistes* (*TLS*, 2002). But for Milton, the Philistines were not a multicultural other, equally legitimate, with a deity that was different but valid; for him, they embraced an evil that had to be eradicated. Samson killed them while they were embracing evil, and his act is meant to be understood as one of heroism, however bloody.

10. See *The Curse of Cain: The Violent Legacy of Monotheism* (Chicago: University of Chicago Press, 1997).

11. Ante-Nicene Christian Library: *Translation of the Writings of the Fathers Down to A.D. 325*, ed. Alexander Roberts and James Donaldson (Edinburgh, 1869), xi. 141–2.

12. Nietzsche, *On the Genealogy of Morals* ed. Douglas Smith (Oxford: Oxford University Press, 2009), First Essay, §14.

13. Alain Badiou, *Ethics: An Essay on the Understanding of Evil*, trans. Peter Hallward (London:Verso, 2002), 70.

14. "Revelation in the Jewish Tradition," in *Beyond the Verse: Talmudic Readings and Lectures*, trans. Gary D. Mole (London: Athlone Press, 1994), 146–7.

15. Some traditions reckon this as the prologue, and in others it is counted as the first commandment.

16. Levinas, "The Temptation of Temptation," in *Nine Talmudic Readings*, trans. Annette Aronowicz (Bloomington: Indiana University Press, 1990), 30–50; p. 37.

17. Levinas, "The Pact," in *Beyond the Verse*, 68–85.

18. In Jacques Derrida's own version of this interiorized justice, this transcendence made immanent, he understands a paradox: "the inaccessible transcendence of the law [*loi*], before which and prior to which man stands fast, only appears infinitely transcendent and thus theological to the extent that, nearest to him, it depends only on him, on the performative act by which he institutes it" (Derrida, *Acts of Religion*, ed. Gil Anidjar, New York: Routledge, 2001, 270. He also writes, "The law is transcendent and theological, and so always to come, always promised, because it is immanent, finite, and thus already past" (270).

19. On the Pauline emphasis on the impartial God, see Wolterstorff's compelling reading of Romans in *Justice in Love* (Grand Rapids: Eerdmans Publishing, 2011), 234–56.

20. Stuart Hampshire, *Justice is Conflict* (Princeton: Princeton University Press, 2000), 4–5.

21. Sandel, "Democracy's Discontent," in *Justice: A Reader*, 330.

22. Levinas, *Beyond the Verse*, 113, my italics.

CHAPTER III. THE POWER OF LOVE

1. Quoted in Louis Adrian Montrose, " 'Eliza, Queene of Shepheardes,' and the Pastoral of Power," in *The Mysteries of Elizabeth I: Selections from English Literary Renaissance*, ed. Kirby Farrell and Kathleen Swaim (Amherst: University of Massachusetts Press, 2003), 165.

2. F. W. Brownlow, "Performance and Reality at the Court of Elizabeth I," ibid. 3.

3. Christine Coch, " 'Mother of my Contreye': Elizabeth I and Tudor Constructions of Motherhood," ibid. 135.

4. Quoted in Kevin Sharpe, *Remapping Early Modern England* (Cambridge: Cambridge University Press, 2000), 110.

5. James I, King of England, *The vvorkes of the most high and mightie prince, Iames by the grace of God, King of Great Britaine, France and Ireland, defender of the faith, &c. Published by Iames, Bishop of Winton, and deane of his Maiesties Chappel Royall* (1616), 1.

6. Scholars have shown that, among other resources, Shakespeare probably read Montaigne's *Essays*, Calvin's *Sermons on Job*, Holinshed's *Chronicles*, and Parson's *Book of Christian Exercise*.

7. All references to the play are to *King Lear*, ed. R. A. Foakes (London: Bloomsbury Arden Shakespeare, 1997). The major intellectual currents of Platonism, Aristotelianism, Stoicism, Skepticism, and Thomism all flow into English Renaissance discourse and are reflected in the play, along with vitalism, humanism, epicureanism, hermeticism, neo-Platonism, the *politique* tradition, and Protestant and Hebraic political thought.

8. Rowan Williams, "Myself as Stranger: Empathy and Loss," Tanner Lectures, Harvard University, April 2014. Much of what follows constituted my invited formal response to him on that occasion.

9. For an astute treatment of the gestures that point to a better world than the one that prevails in *King Lear*, see James Kearney, "This is Above All Strangeness: *King Lear*, Ethics, and the Phenomenology of Recognition", *Criticism*, 54/3 (Summer 2012), 455–67.

10. Calvin's *Sermons on Job*, 11.

11. Ibid. (italics added).

12. The passage has been considered Hand D since the 1870s, and its attribution to Shakespeare, while controversial, is based on handwriting, spelling, vocabulary, and imagery. See *Shakespeare's Hand in the Play of Sir Thomas More*, ed. Alfred Pollard (1923).

13. Niklas Luhmann, *Love as Passion: The Codification of Intimacy*, trans. Jeremy Gaines and Doris Jones (Cambridge, MA: Harvard University Press, 1986), 20.

14. Paul Siegel, "Christianity and the Religion of Love in Romeo and Juliet," *Shakespeare Quarterly*, 12/4 (Autumn 1961), 371–92; p. 372. All references to the play are to *Romeo and Juliet*, ed. René Weis (London: Bloomsbury Arden Shakespeare, 2012).

15. Ibid. 382.

16. Ibid. 384.

17. Ibid. 383.

18. Alan M. F. Gunn, *The Mirror of Love: A Reinterpretation of "The Romance of the Rose"* (Lubbock: Texas Tech Press, 1952), 212.

19. Jewel, *Works*, 2.1128, 1.1129.

20. Daniel Swift, *Shakespeare's Common Prayers* (Oxford: Oxford University Press, 1977), 87.

21. Denis de Rougemont has explored this topos of love and death in *Love in the Western World* (Princeton: Princeton University Press, 1983).

22. Pierre Rousselot, *The Problem of Love in the Middle Ages*, trans. Alan Vincelette (Milwaukee: Marquette University Press, 2002), 79.
23. Siegel, "Christianity and the Religion of Love," 385.
24. In. Di. Nom. C. 4, 1.9 (Frette, v. XXIX, p. 452).
25. *Quodlibetal Questions 1 and 2*, trans. Sandra Edwards, 1.Q.4, A.3 (Toronto: Pontifical Institute of Medieval Studies, 1983), 48.

CHAPTER IV. THE ECONOMICS OF LOVE

1. Geoffrey Claussen, "Sharing the Burden: Rabbi Simḥah Zissel Ziv on Love and Empathy," *Journal of the Society of Christian Ethics*, 30/2 (2010), 153. Claussen discusses this theme at greater length in his book, *Sharing the Burden: Rabbi Simḥah Zissel Ziv and the Path of Musar* (Albany: SUNY Press, 2015), ch. 5.
2. Claussen, "Sharing the Burden," 153.
3. Ibid. 154–5.
4. Ibid. 155.
5. Blaxton, *The English Usurer or Usury Condemned* (London, 1634), 11.
6. Richard Baxter, *Chapters from a Christian Directory*, ed. J. H. Tawney (London, 1925), 106.
7. Muldrew, *The Economy of Obligation*, 126.
8. Thomas Wilson, *The Arte of Rhetorique*, ed. Thomas J. Derrick (London, 1982), 67, 69.
9. Ibid. 71.
10. Elyot, *The Boke Named the Governour, I–II*, ed. Henry Herbert Steven Croft (London, 1880), ii. 201–3, 257–8, spelling modernized.
11. Claussen, "Sharing the Burden," 155.
12. Geoffrey Claussen tells me that Simḥah Zissel did teach in Latvia (in the town of Grobina) for a number of years (1880–6)!
13. It isn't this simple (it never is). A bit of research and I learned that this Musar movement was not all love and all giving, but also had some leaders endorse self-denial, especially later ones, like Yosef Yozel Horowitz, of the school of Novorodok, who focused on the sinfulness and lowliness of the human being. Indeed, the entry in the *Encyclopaedia Britannia* on the Musar is harsh, emphasizing that the movement was a pietist one of self-discipline and Torah study in contrast to a movement focused on ethics. That was not my family. Claussen also discusses these themes of self-denial and sinfulness in *Sharing the Burden*.
14. As Claussen explains in *Sharing the Burden*, ch. 2, Simḥah Zissel often depicted human beings as inclined towards evil, "but he also acknowledges an intrinsically good side to human nature which must be nurtured."
15. Ian Baucom, "Amicus Curiae": The Friend, the Enemy, and the Politics of Love," *PMLA* 124/5 (October 2009), 1717.

16. Quoted in Claussen, *Sharing the Burden*, ch. 2.

17. Claussen, *Sharing the Burden*, 156.

18. Jeff Ferriell, *Understanding Contracts*, 2nd edn. (New Providence, NJ: Matthew Bender and Co., 2009), 1.

19. John Rawls, *A Theory of Justice* (Cambridge, MA: Harvard University Press, 1971), 11.

20. Ibid. 12–13.

21. Michael Sandel, *Liberalism and the Limits of Justice* (Cambridge: Cambridge University Press, 1998),107.

22. Ibid.

23. Ibid. 114. The Uniform Commercial Code of the United States has adopted a doctrine of "unconscionability," wherein contracts that are based on extreme procedural or substantive unfairness are not binding.

24. Ibid. 110.

25. As J. L. Austin demonstrated in *How to Do Things with Words* (Oxford: Oxford University Press, 1955) a performative utterance requires felicitous conditions.

26. *The Human Condition* (Chicago: University of Chicago Press, 1958), 237.

27. Despite the bluntness of the instrument of the law, the most sophisticated legal scholars have carefully noted the limitations of contractual models. Ian McNeil has observed that "few economic exchanges occur entirely in the discrete transactional pattern." "The entangling strings of friendship, reputation, interdependence, morality and altruistic desires are integral parts of the relation…" ("Restatement (Second) of Contracts and Presentation," *Virginia Law Review*, 60 (1974), 589-610; p. 595).

28. Richmond Noble, *Shakespeare's Biblical Knowledge* (New York: The Society for Promoting Christian Knowledge, 1935), 97. All references to the play are to *The Merchant of Venice*, ed. John Drakakis (London: Bloomsbury Arden Shakespeare, 2010).

29. Ibid. 66.

30. On this reading, equity courts are an effective mechanism to grant clemency while a strict adherence to a contract looks less forgiving: a court of equity may well forgive the penalty clause of a pound of flesh, but Shylock anticipates that the Venetian court will enforce it. *Pacta sunt servanda*, promises are meant to be kept: there is a moral duty to keep one's word. This explains why in civil law, contrary to common law, the typical remedy for breach of contract is specific performance instead of damages. "To ensure that the promisor will fulfill his end of the bargain, the civil law not only allows, but also encourages the addition of a penalty precisely to do what the common law abhors: to compel performance… To make this point clear, Article 1226 of the French Civil Code defines a penalty as '[A] clause by which a person, in order to ensure the performance of an agreement, promises something in case such agreement is not performed [by him]'" (*Louisiana Law review*, Vol. 60, p. 1093).

31. Noble, *Shakespeare's Biblical Knowledge*, 243. John Coolidge summarizes, "The Law, justice, and their concomitant 'wisdom' are not simply rejected, then. What is rejected is their finality. They must be bound to love. To choose that love is to find their true meaning, but to choose them without love is to be a 'deliberate fool.'" Sounds good, but this is ultimately, as its author confesses at the start, a reading of *The Merchant* as "a work of Christian apologetics"—and perhaps too of "equity apologetics."

32. Daniel J. Kornstein, *Kill All the Lawyers? Shakespeare's Legal Appeal* (Princeton: Princeton University Press, 1994), 81.

33. Sandra Day O'Connor was referred to as "the Portia who now graces our [Supreme] Court," ibid.

34. Ibid. 76.

35. John Kerrigan has offered a hair-raising account of the anti-Semitic charges permeating discourse during the Renaissance, from making ungodly oaths to not keeping promises, from injuring Christians without remorse to murdering Christ and Christians. See *Shakespeare's Binding Language* (Oxford: Oxford University Press, 2016).

36. Mark Edwin Andrews, *Law versus Equity in "The Merchant of Venice"* (Boulder: University of Colorado Press, 1965); Maxine McKay, "*The Merchant of Venice*: A Reflection of the Early Conflict between Courts of Law and Courts of Equity," *Shakespeare Quarterly*, 15 (1964), 371–5; W. Nicholas Knight, "Shakespeare's Court Case," *Law and Critique*, 2 (1991), 103–12.

37. Stephen A. Cohen, "'The Quality of Mercy': Law, Equity and Ideology in *The Merchant of Venice*," *Mosaic*, 27/4 (December 1994), 38.

38. Ibid. 40.

39. This she does by recourse to the old Alien Statute of Venice, a statute that allows the state to take all of the property of an alien who makes not only direct but also "indirect attempts" on the life of any citizen—and even to execute him.

40. Roger Strittmater, *Notes and Queries*, 245/1 (March 2000), 71.

41. On his portrayal of the Jews, see James Shapiro, *Shakespeare and the Jews* (New York: Columbia University Press, 1997). See also David M. Posner "Religious Economies in *The Merchant of Venice*," in *Annals of Scholarship* 16:1–3 (2004): 139–53.

42. This solution is the subject of much debate. Jacques Derrida has written about the dangers that lurk in the globalization of insincere apology.

43. In his *Philosophy of Right*, Hegel describes the development in the midst of ethical life of a "system of needs" of a domain of economic activity governed by commodity exchange and the pursuit of economic self-interest. And for him, the emergence of this sphere means the disappearance of the common concern for association, for the *res publica*, from the hearts and minds of men (*Hegel's Philosophy of Right*, trans. T. M. Knox, Oxford: Oxford University Press, 1973), 126.

44. Posner fails to distinguish positive economics from efficiency, consequently eliding the important difference between the work of legislators and judges,

makers of policy and upholders of law, and his debt to utilitarianism is far deeper than his superficial distinction would have it—he substitutes the maximization of wealth for the maximization of happiness. John M. Buchanan, "Good Economics, Bad Law," *Virginia Law Review*, 60/3 (March 1974), 483–92; John T. Noonan, Jr., "Posner's Problematics," *Harvard Law Review*, 111/7 (May 1998), 1768–75; Thomas Sharpe, Review of *The Economics of Justice*, *The Economic Journal* 93/369 (March 1983), 248–9, among others.

45. Richard Posner, *The Economics of Justice* (Cambridge, MA: Harvard University Press, 1981), 67–8.

46. Claussen, "Sharing the Burden," 155.

CHAPTER V. THE FORGIVENESS OF LOVE

1. Immanuel Kant, *Groundwork of the Metaphysics of Morals* (1785), trans. Mary Gregor (Cambridge: Cambridge University Press, 1997), 19.

2. Carol S. Steiker, "Murphy on Mercy: A Prudential Reconsideration," *Criminal Justice Ethics*, 27/2 (Summer–Fall 2008), 45–54, 49.

3. Ibid.

4. Herbert Morris, "Persons and Punishments," 1968, in *On Guilt and Innocence: Essays in Legal Philosophy and Moral Psychology* (Berkeley: University of California Press, 1976).

5. I am referring to *The Republic*, which is admittedly Plato's idealistic outlook on justice. He takes up the question of punishment in *Gorgias*, *Laws*, and *Protagoras* with different purposes. Summarizing them, Mary MacKenzie concludes: "Despite such differences, the penal theory to be found in these four dialogues remains constant. It centres on the principle of reform, whose objective is to make the criminal virtuous, for his own benefit" (Mary Margaret MacKenzie, *Plato on Punishment* (Berkeley: University of California Press, 1981), 204–5.

6. *Republic*, trans. Allan Bloom (New York: Basic Books, 1968), 335e.

7. Richard Posner, *The Economics of Justice* (Cambridge, MA: Harvard University Press, 1981).

8. Robert Nozick, *Philosophical Explanations* (Cambridge, MA: Harvard University Press, 1981), 370.

9. Ibid. 372.

10. Ibid. 374.

11. Jeffrie G. Murphy, *Getting Even: Forgiveness and its Limits* (Oxford and New York: Oxford University Press, 2003), 13.

12. *Montaigne's Essays*, trans. John Florio, ed. L. C. Harmer, 3 vols (London: Everyman's Library, 1965), book 2, section 11.

13. This is what the Truth and Reconciliation Commission in South Africa seeks.

14. Louis E. Newman, *Past Imperatives: Studies in the History and Theory of Jewish Ethics* (Albany: SUNY Press, 1998), 94.

15. Ibid. 45.
16. The Catholic Encyclopedia online, "penance."
17. Radically, Hannah Arendt argues that God follows the human initiative of forgiveness when He forgives us. Either way, human and divine forgiveness are linked (*The Human Condition*, 239).
18. It turns out that unwillingness characterizes all of the major prophets after all, beginning with Moses, who all demur when they are given an assignment to deliver the bad news. "But I am slow of speech," claims the hesitant Moses; "But I do not know how to speak, I am only a child," says the demurring Jeremiah; "I am lost for I am a man of unclean lips," complains the reluctant Isaiah.
19. Newman, *Past Imperatives*, 90.
20. "Standing injustice" is explored helpfully by Dan Philpott in *Just and Unjust Peace: An Ethic of Political Reconciliation* (Oxford: Oxford University Press, 2012).
21. The contemporary philosopher, Raimond Gaita, concurs on the importance of manifesting guilt and shame, which "often express acknowledgement of collective responsibility, sometimes directly for the wrongs done, but more often to those who were wronged by our political ancestors. It amounts to the acknowledgement that we are rightly called to a communal responsiveness to those who are the victims of wrongdoing or the wrongdoing of those who preceded us" (Raimond Gaita, *A Common Humanity: Thinking about Love and Truth and Justice* (London and New York: Routledge, 2000), 87).
22. Emmanuel Levinas, *Entre nous: On Thinking-of-the-other*, trans. Michael B. Smith and Barbara Harshav (New York: Columbia University Press, 1998), 108.
23. Ibid. 107.
24. Derrida writes, "Forgiveness of the unforgivable (and that is the only proper meaning of forgiveness for him) does not exist as possible, it only exists by exempting itself from the law of the possible" (in *Questioning God*, ed. John Caputo, Mark Dooley, and Michael Scanlon, Bloomington: Indiana University Press, 2001).
25. Timothy Jackson, *Priority of Love* (Princeton: Princeton University Press, 2003), 141.
26. All references to the play are to *Hamlet*, ed. Ann Thompson and Neil Taylor (London: Bloomsbury Arden Shakespeare, 2006). Preface to Shakespeare in *The Yale Edition of the Works of Samuel Johnson* (New Haven: Yale University Press, 1958–90), viii. 1011.
27. See the excellent discussion of *Hamlet* in Brian Cummings, *Mortal Thoughts: Religion, Secularity, and Identity in Shakespeare and Early Modern Culture* (Oxford: Oxford University Press, 2013).
28. Margreta de Grazia's *Hamlet Without Hamlet* (Cambridge: Cambridge University Press, 2007) focuses on inheritance. Gabriel Josipovici has

written a rich discussion of the irresolvable echoes in *Hamlet: Fold on Fold* (New Haven: Yale University Press, 2016). William Kerrigan's *Hamlet's Perfection* (Baltimore: Johns Hopkins University Press, 1996) mines its Senecan traditions.

29. Quentin Skinner, in *Forensic Shakespeare* (Oxford: Oxford University Press, 2014), has demonstrated the play's debt to judicial rhetoric.

30. Newman, *Past Imperatives*, 90, my italics.

31. Jeffrie Murphy, "Legal Moralism and Retribution Revisited", *The Proceedings and Addresses of the American Philosophical Association*, 80/2 (November 2006), 45–62, 46.

32. Compare Murphy, *Getting Even*, 46.

33. Arendt understood Jesus of Nazareth, the human Jesus, as a great spokesman for this kind of forgiveness that enables a new beginning. See *The Human Condition*, 238.

34. John Milbank "Forgiveness and Incarnation," in *Questioning God*, 2–128; 102.

35. John Kerrigan has shown how the play's energies are marshaled for remembering the Ghost rather than avenging. See *Revenge Tragedy: Aeschylus to Armageddon* (Oxford: Oxford University Press, 1998).

36. Eleanor Prosser, *Hamlet and Revenge* (Stanford: Stanford University Press, 1967), 5.

37. Edwin Sandys, *Certaine sermons or Homilies, appointed to be read in churches, in the time of Queen Elizabeth I, 1547–1571*, 2 vols in 1 (Gainesville, FL: Scholars' Facsimiles and Reprints, 1968), Homily 12, 1. 93.

38. Prosser, *Hamlet and Revenge*, 4.

39. Prosser convincingly shows how the scene in *Henry V* which many regard as retributive—in which Henry doles out his punishments to those who plotted to murder their king (2.2.12–181)—is the opposite: Henry exacts repentance from his plotters, thankfulness that their purposes have been prevented, and joy in their contrition.

40. Prosser, *Hamlet and Revenge*, 82.

41. Sarah Beckwith points to the language of acknowledgement bound up with confession, *Shakespeare and the Grammar of Forgiveness* (Ithaca: Cornell University Press, 2011), 2. As David Steinmetz argues, the Reformation began in a debate about the meaning of penitence: not a set of actions (the *agite poenitentiam* of the Vulgate) but a change of heart, repentance as metanoia, turning toward God. David Steinmetz, "Reformation and Grace," in *Grace upon Grace: Essays in Honor of Thomas A. Langford*, ed. Robert K. Johnston, Gregory Jones, and Jonathan R. Wilson (Nashville: Abingdon Press, 1999).

42. Piero Boitani, *The Gospel According to Shakespeare*, trans. Vittorio Montemaggi and Rachel Jacoff (Notre Dame: University of Notre Dame Press, 2013), 8.

43. Ibid. 36.

44. All references to the play are to *The Tempest*, ed. Virginia Mason Vaughan and Alden T. Vaughan (London: Bloomsbury Arden Shakespeare, 1999). Sarah Beckwith has written on forgiveness in Shakespeare's late romances. "The late romances explore the vulnerabilities, exposures, and commitments of forgiving and being forgiven in new forms of theater charged with finding the pathways and possibilities of forgiveness in the absence of auricular confession and priestly absolution" (*Shakespeare and the Grammar of Forgiveness*, 2).

45. Paul rehearses this teaching in Romans 12:14-17: "Bless those who persecute you, bless and do not curse them...Do not repay anyone evil for evil, but take thought for what is noble in the sight of all." And in his first letter to the Thessalonians: "See that none of you repays evil for evil, but always seek to do good to one another and to all (5:15).

46. This does not prevent Christ from feeling moral indignation against wrong. See also Matt. 5:29-30 and 23:33, Luke 13:1-5.

AFTERWORD

1. Michael Sandel, "Democracy's Discontents," in *Justice: A Reader*, 331.

Index